Atlas of Improbable Places

TRAVIS ELBOROUGH is an author and social commentator. His books include *A Traveller's Year*, *A London Year*, *The Long-Player Goodbye*, *Being A Writer* and *A Walk in the Park: The Life and Times of a People's Institution*. Travis is a regular contributor to Radio 4 and the *Guardian*, and has penned articles on all aspects of travel and culture, from pirates in the Caribbean to donkeys at the British seaside. He has written for the *Times*, *Sunday Times*, *New Statesman*, *BBC History Magazine* and *Kinfolk* among others.

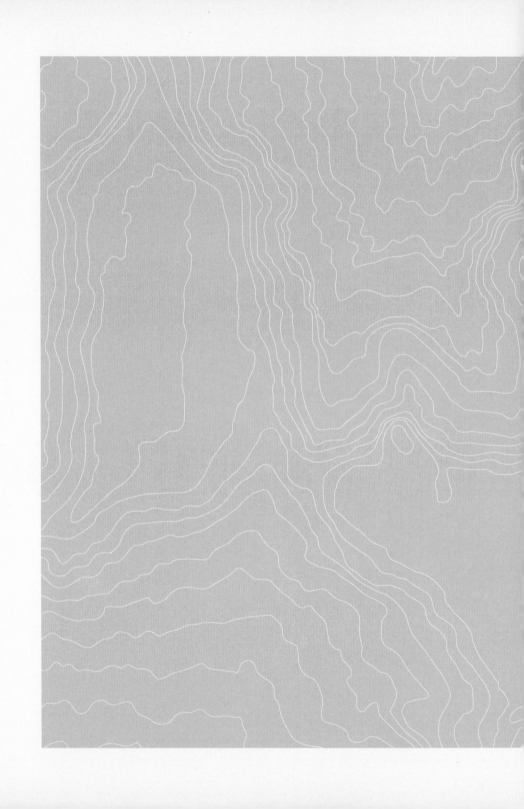

Atlas of Improbable Places

A journey to the world's most unusual corners

Travis Elborough
& Alan Horsfield

1	FLEVOPOLDER	14	HUMBERSTONE AND SANTA LAURA
2	ZHELEZNOGORSK	15	WONDERLAND
3	FREE CHRISTIANIA	16	ORADOUR-SUR-GLANE
4	AUROVILLE	17	MUYNAK
5	SLAB CITY	18	WITTENOOM
6	PORTMEIRION	19	ANI, KARS
7	ZVYOZDNY GORODOK	20	CONCRETE CITY
8	HEARST CASTLE	21	VAROSHA
9	TEUFELSBERG	22	MARYHILL STONEHENGE
10	PRESIDIO MODELO	23	SPIJKENISSE
11	BATTLESHIP ISLAND	24	KABAYAN
12	NO MAN'S LAND FORT	25	SANTURIO MADONNA DELLA CORONA
13	THE LOST CITY OF SAN JUAN PARANGARICUTIRO	26	LONDON BRIDGE, LAKE HAVASU

CONTENTS

INTRODUCTION

Maps, the great Italian writer Italo Calvino once maintained, presuppose the idea of a narrative because they are conceived on the basis of a journey, an odyssey. The earliest need to fix places on stone, skin or primitive paper was fundamentally linked to travel and the earliest cartographers looked to the sky rather than the earth for their starting points of reference. Today heavenly bodies, arguably, still guide us, as we take directions from GPS systems beaming information from satellites orbiting our planet. But the gulf between the age of the sextant and the wooden sailing ship, when so much of the world remained uncharted territory, and our satellite navigation-enabled present, seems impossibly vast.

To travel back then was often to embark on a journey into the unknown, with the final destination vague or the subject of wild speculation if not outright fiction, and one which the voyager might never reach let alone return from. We are, of course, the lucky beneficiaries of such sometimes suicidal pioneering expeditions. Places that were once the stuff of dreams and improbable to the point of implausibility are as accessible and now almost as familiar to us as our own neighbourhoods. Though that is not without its downsides entirely. Few of us believe the world is flat. But an hour or so on Google Maps or TripAdvisor surveying an increasingly interconnected and corporately globalized planet can definitely make us feel that it is flatter. Or at least rather less fantastical and strange than it was for our ancestors: a case of 'here be dragons' on the far corner of a sketchily drawn map giving way to 'here be some well-known brands and chain shops' flagged upon arrival on your phone's app.

It was Calvino again who over forty years ago, in *Invisible Cities*, presciently invented a fictional metropolis called Trude whose overwhelming characteristic is that it is exactly the same as everywhere else. 'If on arriving at Trude I had not read the city's name written in big letters,' the story's narrator states, 'I would have thought I was landing at the same airport from which I had taken off.' At the end of the tale, his traveller, bored by Trude's similarity with so many other places, begs to leave but is informed they will only 'arrive at another Trude, absolutely the same, detail by detail. The world is covered by a sole Trude which does not begin and does not end. Only the name of the airport changes.'

But claims about the growing, soul-crushing similarity of places can be overstated, as hopefully this volume illustrates. Thankfully, the world continues to be a dizzyingly diverse place. Our appetite for the unusual and the out of the ordinary has, if anything, only been heightened by new technology, the scanning and sharing of fresh information and imagery themselves a spur to further travel, and post-industrialization changing the kinds of places we find intriguing, beautiful or worthy of cursory investigation. When almost every action we perform online is tracked and all things digital attempt to distance us from the body and physical disintegration, it's perhaps not so surprising that our fascination with the utterly abandoned, the long unobserved, the decayed and ruined has increased exponentially. That pictures of a weed-infested factory or decaying mansion in Detroit or St Louis, say, will frequently have their greatest currency on Instagram or other social media sites, only reaffirms rather than contradicts a particular contemporary desire to seek out the obscure and the unburnished.

The Atlas of Improbable Places, then, is intended as a compendium of unlikely, curious and plain odd locales. The improbability factor, if you will, of each of these places was that they were distinguished by some element of their architecture, natural geography or present or past state of being. Improbability may have been inherent at the beginning, or thrust upon them later or only accrued in recent times, but these places all have stories to tell us. The map may not be the territory, just as written history is not the sum of any individual place. But ideally we need to read them both to reach a greater understanding of where we are and where we might be going.

DREAM CREATIONS

Flevopolder

The region reclaimed from the sea

Lelystad [Netherlands]

52° 30' 0" N
5° 28' 0" E

For nearly 2,000 years, the occupants of what is today the Netherlands have been locked into an almost Sisyphean battle to hold back and reclaim land from the sea. Traces of this struggle can be detected in the remains of ancient *terpen*, or earth mounds, that still survive in certain parts of the country. Dating from around 500 BC these edifices, along with earthen dykes, served as the most basic bulwark against flooding for the earliest settlers to these often sodden lands. But such defences alone could hardly be expected to halt the advances of a rampaging North Sea, and a series of particularly savage storms in the eleventh and twelfth centuries led to the deaths from drowning of tens of thousands and water permanently claiming huge swathes of the northern coast. One beneficiary of these topographical changes, however, was the estuary town of Amsterdam, which suddenly found itself with a direct route to the ocean and subsequently developed into a major port and finally wound up as the capital city.

Still, the story of this country, over half of which presently lies below sea level, is as much about land gain as loss. God, it is said, may have created the world, but the Dutch gave the world the Netherlands. Around 10 per cent of the whole country is made up of bits that were once under water. And much of the rest of it would be, too, but for an extensive network of canals, dams, drains and dykes that were begun in the Middle Ages. By the fifteenth century, the Dutch had developed a highly sophisticated hydro-engineering system, one that involved using encircling dykes and water-pumping windmills – hence their ubiquity in this landscape – to drain quite substantial tranches of saturated ground and complete ponds,

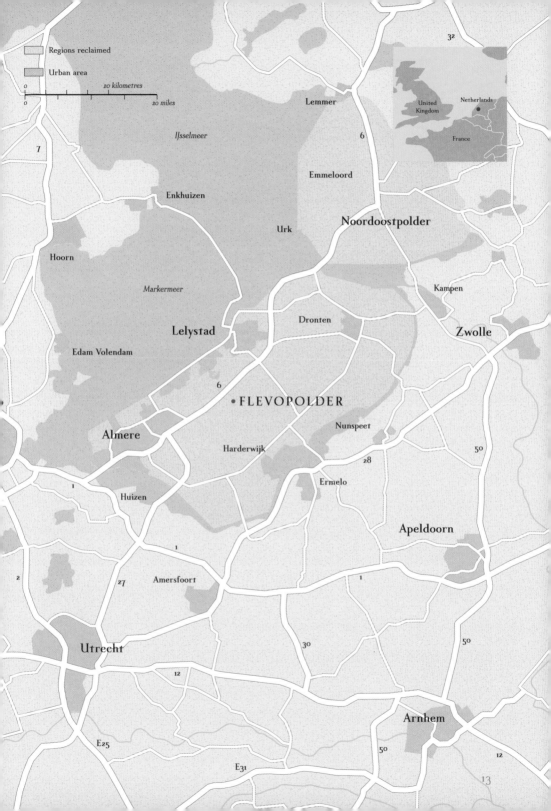

Regions reclaimed
Urban area

0
20 kilometres
0
20 miles

IJsselmeer

Lemmer

6

Emmeloord

Noordoostpolder

Enkhuizen

Urk

Kampen

Hoorn

Markermeer

Dronten

Zwolle

Lelystad

Edam Volendam

6

•FLEVOPOLDER

Almere

Nunspeet

50

Harderwijk

28

Huizen

Ermelo

1

Apeldoorn

1

1

Amersfoort

2

27

30

50

Utrecht

12

Arnhem

E25

50

12

E31

32

United Kingdom

Netherlands

France

7

13

rivers and lakes. The resulting drained lands, known as *polders*, could then be used for farming and building on. This technique would reach its pinnacle in the latter half of the twentieth century with the creation of Flevoland, a cluster of polders that make up the Netherland's twelfth and newest province. It is also the world's largest artificial island.

Flevoland represents the fulfilment of an ambition, long held by Dutch civil engineers, to tame the Zuider Zee, or South Sea. Once an estuary of the River Rhine, it had, through storms and by a process of natural erosion, become an inland sea that seemed bent only on further extending its extent. The first proposal to close it off and drain the land came in 1667 from the pioneering hydraulicist Henric Stevin, who stated his objective as being to rid the Netherlands of 'the fury and the poison of the North Sea . . . together with all the brackish waters from Seeland, Hollant and West-Frieslant'. His dream, alas, came to nothing and the idea was shelved until the nineteenth century when steam-powered water pumps looked set to make his idea a much more viable proposition. But nearly thirty plans

Below: New towns mushrooming where once there was water.

were published before the baton was picked up in the 1890s by Cornelius Lely. A former student of engineering at the Polytechnic School of Delft, Lely was the Minister of Transport and Water Management who prepared several technical reports and became a fervent advocate for a reclamation scheme. Nevertheless, government approval was granted only in the wake of another terrible flood in 1916 and the first stage of Zuider Zee works started in 1920 when construction began on the Afsluitdijk. This nineteen-mile-long dyke was to connect the provinces of Noord-Holland and Friesland and seal off the Zuider Zee from the Wadden Zee (Mud Sea) and the North Sea. With its completion in 1932, the Zuider Zee ceased to exist, its briny waters soon replaced by freshwater from the IJssel River amid the formation of artificial freshwater lake, the IJsselmeer. This part of the scheme was greeted with dismay by the region's trawlermen, who railed against the loss of direct access to the sea and fish stocks.

Over the next four decades, though, thousands of square metres of land were drained in stages, to produce the group of *polders* that since 1986 have comprised the Flevoland province. Earlier reclamations were mostly about agriculture, but here two new planned cities, Lelystad (named in honour of Cornelius Lely) and Almere, have arisen. If not without their detractors (one guidebook dismisses both cities as 'grindingly dull places, laid out in unrelieved grid patterns'), Almere, whose population was just 100,000 in 1997 and today is close to double that, is the fastest growing city in the Netherlands. Among its assets are fascinating pieces of contemporary public art and examples of modern architecture, including Marinus Boezem's Groene Kathedraal (Green Cathedral), an arrangement of Italian poplar trees grown over thirty years to the plan of the cathedral of Notre-Dame de Reims, and the 'Fantasy' district of temporary experimental environmental housing. The latter dates from an original competition in 1982 which called on artists, engineers, architects and even members of the public to submit designs for imaginatively 'unusual living' spaces.

ZHELEZNOGORSK

FORMER CLOSED SOVIET CITY

SIBERIA [RUSSIA]

56° 15' 16"N
93° 32' 0"E

Secrecy is everything with Zheleznogorsk. Known for decades by the postal code name Krasnoyarsk-26 and not appearing on any public maps, the city was founded on the banks of the Yenisei River in 1950 as a centre for plutonium production and was not officially acknowledged until 1992.

In keeping with Comrade Stalin's scheme to create a secret network of regional technical centres to produce and develop material for the Soviet Union's military arsenal, Zheleznogorsk was a purpose-built closed city, a place so separate that it boasted its own flag featuring a bear wrestling, bare-pawed, with a nuclear atom. Foreign nationals were forbidden to enter it and it was out of bounds to most Russian citizens, too. Even the top-flight graduates and scientists who were recruited to live and work in Zheleznogorsk had to seek special permission to leave it. Any relatives wishing to visit them there were carefully vetted before being granted admission. Despite these restrictions and its remote Siberian location, it was considered a prestigious posting in the communist era. Perks included better food and the esteem of those in the know for developing such capitalist-beating space-age gizmos as the Kosmos and Molniya communication satellites.

After the fall of the Berlin Wall in 1989 and the subsequent break-up of the Soviet Union, Zheleznogorsk's fortunes took a tumble. But following fresh government investment in the 2000s, the city received a new lease of life, and was involved in the development of Russia's answer to America's Global Positioning Satellite (GPS): the Glonass satellite navigation system.

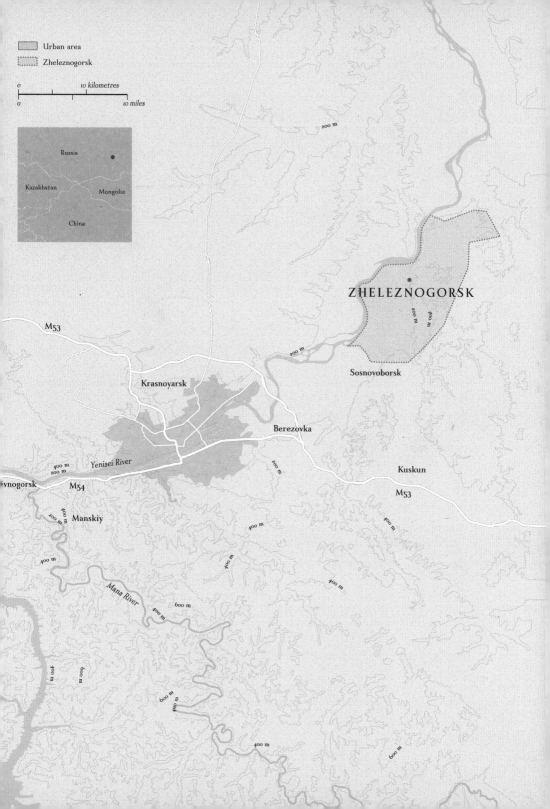

Urban area
Zheleznogorsk

0   10 kilometres
0   10 miles

Russia

Kazakhstan

Mongolia

China

200 m

ZHELEZNOGORSK

M53

200 m

200 m

400 m

Krasnoyarsk

Sosnovoborsk

Berezovka

200 m

Kuskun

400 m

200 m

vnogorsk

M54

M53

400 m

Manskiy

Yenisei River

400 m

200 m

400 m

400 m

400 m

400 m

Mana River

600 m

400 m

400 m

600 m

600 m

400 m

400 m

600 m

Today its main factory and research laboratories produce navigation, telecommunications and geodetic satellites for local and overseas clients, including Indonesia and Israel, all the while continuing to tinker with numerous top-secret projects for the Russian military.

Retaining its 1950s 'Motherland' cinema and regimented rows of functional five-storey housing blocks, Zheleznogorsk could be taken for a

vintage Soviet theme park. If time has not stood still here entirely, access
to the plants remains restricted and its prized, well-remunerated resident
workers' comings and goings continue to be monitored: notice must be
given before departing from, or returning to, the city.

Free Christiania

Squatter-city
Copenhagen [Denmark]

55° 40' 33" N
12° 36' 29" E

There are many routes to freedom. Back in 1971, though, Copenhagen's number 8 bus was advertised as offering the most direct one yet, as it carried eager liberty-seekers straight to Christiania – the self-declared 'free city' in a corner of the Danish capital.

Coming into being when a group of protesters occupied an abandoned army barracks by the canal, Christiania was a child of the hippie movement and student activism of the late 1960s. Anti-authoritarian to its core, its stated mission was 'to be a self-governing society . . . self-sustaining . . . and aspiring to avert psychological and physical destitution'. Rejecting the materialist mores of what was deemed the 'straight society', its founders were for both marijuana and macrobiotic diets but frowned on private property and bourgeois convention.

Of course, in the early 1970s such an outlook was itself fairly conventional, at least among the young. Many in that era experimented with communal living and free love, took up macramé, thought Jim Morrison of the Doors was a poet, baked their own bread, wore their hair long and favoured cheesecloth clothing.

But where most other squats and anarchic enclaves of a similar ilk gradually fell victim to the law, infighting, infiltration by miscreants and the passing of flower power fashions, Christiania has endured for more than four decades. In all that time, it has acted as a sanctuary for artists, musicians, film-makers, naturists, crafters, actors, underground theatre folk, Marxists, Zen Buddhists and new age therapists, if also correspondingly attracting Hell's Angels, cranks and the odd out and out crook.

Nyholm

Frederiksholm

Kobenhavns Havn

Arsenaloen

Prinsessegade

• FREE
CHRISTIANIA

Christiania
Blacksmith

Strandgade

Wildersgade

Christianshavns Kanal

Christianshavn

Dronningensgade

Torvegade

Kaninoen

Stadagraven

Vermlandsgade

Amager Blvd.

Store Kongensgade

Bredgade

O2

O2

Norway

Sweden

Denmark

Germany

Urban area

0
200 metres

0
200 yards

Today, Christiania is Copenhagen's second most popular tourist destination. A green and pleasant, bustling, car-free, eighty-four-acre waterside settlement, Christiania is comprised of brightly painted wooden huts amid leafy gardens, and reclaimed military and industrial buildings plastered with lurid murals. Eight hundred people call it home and meet weekly to decide every necessary course of action collectively. It has its own currency, and there are playgrounds and allotments, art galleries, performance spaces, workshops, vegetarian cafés, jazz and rock clubs, bars, shops and stalls selling organic groceries, crafts, jewellery and vintage clothes. Its continued survival, though, has frequently hung in the balance and its relationship with the Danish state has often been fraught.

Throughout its existence, perhaps the thorniest issue has always been the open buying and selling of cannabis on Christiania's main thoroughfare, its famed Pusher Street. Cannabis is illegal in Denmark. Its consumption is considered practically a fundamental right, on the other hand, within the free city itself. For years, the Danish authorities tacitly turned a blind eye to cannabis here, as long as hard drugs were kept out. For a while, Christiania was even officially classed as 'a social experiment' and largely left to its own devices. But disputes between rival biker gangs over control of the cannabis trade, coupled with a steady rise in the price of property in Copenhagen, led in 2004 to the government drawing up proposals to end Christiania's anomalous status. In the event, a compromise was reached, and, a decade later, its residents were given the right to buy the land at below market rates. While opposing the very idea of private property on principle, they chose to exercise this option communally. Christiania was then put into the hands of a foundation, and its integrity and its manner of life left mostly intact.

Right: The gateway to freedom at Christiania; The town remains free, though its heyday was in the 1970s.

AUROVILLE

1960s UTOPIAN CITY
PONDICHERRY [INDIA]

12° 0' 19" N
79° 48' 46" E

If anyone ever decided to invent an architectural category called mystical modernism, Auroville could arguably fit the bill. The result of a vision of an Indian promoter of 'integral yoga' and a plan by a French disciple of Le Corbusier, this 'international city' at Pondicherry in Tamil Nadu, southern India, was inaugurated in 1968 and then optimistically expected to attract some 50,000 residents. Currently about 2,500 live there permanently, the majority from North America and Europe.

The idea for this settlement, an attempt to build a spiritual utopia free from rules, money and leaders, grew out of an ashram established there by Sri Aurobindo. Aurobindo was a Cambridge-educated Eastern philosopher and campaigner for Indian independence who turned to Hindu scriptures during his internment for sedition by the British in 1908.

Withdrawing into his room in Pondicherry in 1926 and dying twenty-four years later, Aurobindo entrusted the running of the ashram to one of his most loyal followers, Mirra Alfassa. Known as 'the Mother', Alfassa dreamed of creating a new kind of city, 'a place . . . of collaboration and real brotherhood' to be named Auroville in Aurobindo's honour.

She secured the backing of the Indian government and UNESCO, and the architect Roger Anger was employed to draw up a scheme. His starting point was a sketch by the Mother which divided the city up into four separate zones for industry, culture, housing and international pavilions, respectively. Taking his cue from the whorl of a galaxy, Anger suggested a radial arrangement with an assortment of white block buildings spinning out from a main green space.

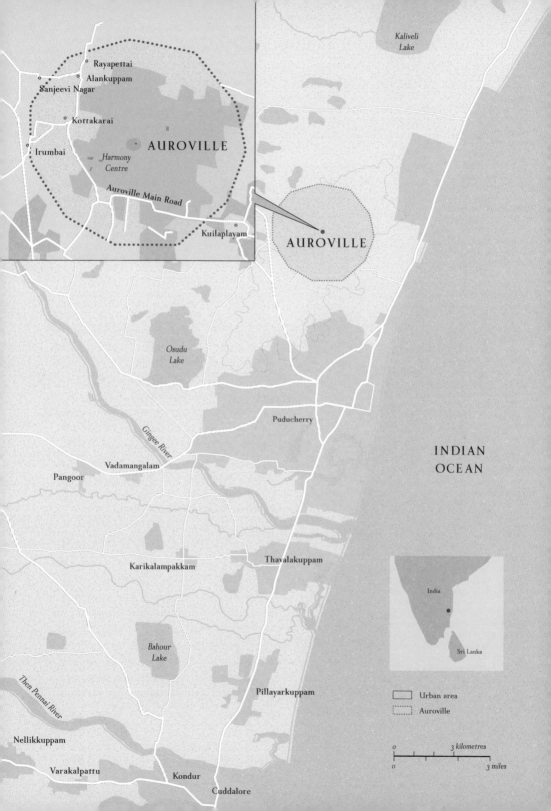

Rayapettai
Alankuppam
Sanjeevi Nagar
Kottakarai
Irumbai
Harmony Centre

AUROVILLE

Auroville Main Road
Kuilaplayam

Kaliveli Lake

AUROVILLE

Osudu Lake

Gingee River

Puducherry

Vadamangalam

Pangoor

INDIAN OCEAN

Karikalampakkam

Thavalakuppam

India

Sri Lanka

Bahour Lake

Then Pennai River

Pillayarkuppam

Nellikkuppam

Varakalpattu   Kondur

Cuddalore

Urban area
Auroville

0   3 *kilometres*
0   3 *miles*

In the end, these central gardens would always be rather upstaged by the feature at their heart: a giant gold geodesic domed temple, not unlike an oversized golf ball. It is used for meditation and called Matrimandir, and its design was personally chosen by the Mother herself in 1970.

Currently, the city is half powered by solar energy and is as committed as ever to organic farming, recycling and the use of sustainable indigenous building material, though Anger's original layout has been undermined somewhat by the rather ad hoc addition of newer, residential quarters

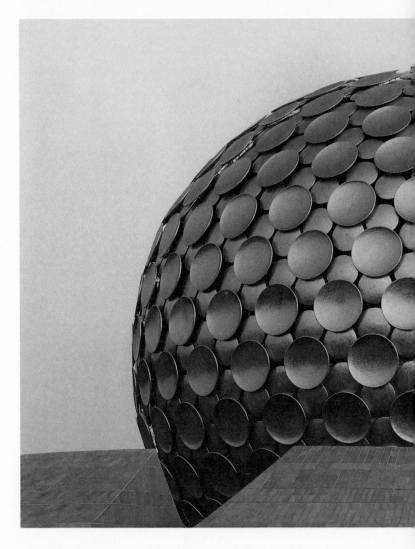

bearing such titles as 'Existence', 'Sincerity', 'Surrender' and 'Invocation'.

Significantly more damaging for Auroville, however, have been reports in more recent years of its failure to tackle serious cases of sexual assault and corruption, and claims that the community exploits the local Tamil labour force. All of which has rather tarnished its reputation as a supposed beacon of peace, love and harmony, no matter how brightly its gold temple glistens under the blazing south Indian sun.

SLAB CITY

THE SQUATTER METROPOLIS

CALIFORNIA [UNITED STATES]

33° 15' 28" N
115° 27' 44" W

The slabs, of course, come as no real surprise, written as they are into this Californian city's somewhat unprepossessing name. The eighteen-hole golf course, on the other hand, is one of the less expected facilities at Slab City, even if its greens are unlikely to give Shinnecock Hills or St Andrews much of a run for their money. Even to use the term 'green' would be overdoing it since the whole course is laid out on the stony scrabble of the Sonoran Desert and completely lacks the sort of foliage that could be trimmed and tamed into anything resembling a lawn. Gamely Slab City players pay no heed to the absence of conditions most golfers would consider normal, if not absolutely essential, for their sport. But if they wanted what passes for normality elsewhere, they wouldn't be in Slab City in the first place – or so some would reason. Year round, there are about 200 residents, their numbers swelled in winter by an influx of migrants in RVs, the so-called snowbirds fleeing the colder climes of the north and Midwest. For them, the beauty of Slab City is that it's not subject to so many of the rules that prevail elsewhere in the United States.

Affectionately known as 'the last free place in America', Slab City is a squatter community 140 miles east of San Diego and 50 miles north of the Mexican border. Occupying 640 acres of concrete and debris-littered government land at Camp Dunlop (an abandoned marine training base that is still fringed by a fully operational army firing range), its citizens live rent-free in makeshift homes ingeniously fashioned from scrap, old cars and vans and trailers (some equipped with solar panels), or just tents augmented with planks of wood, pieces of cardboard and blankets. The

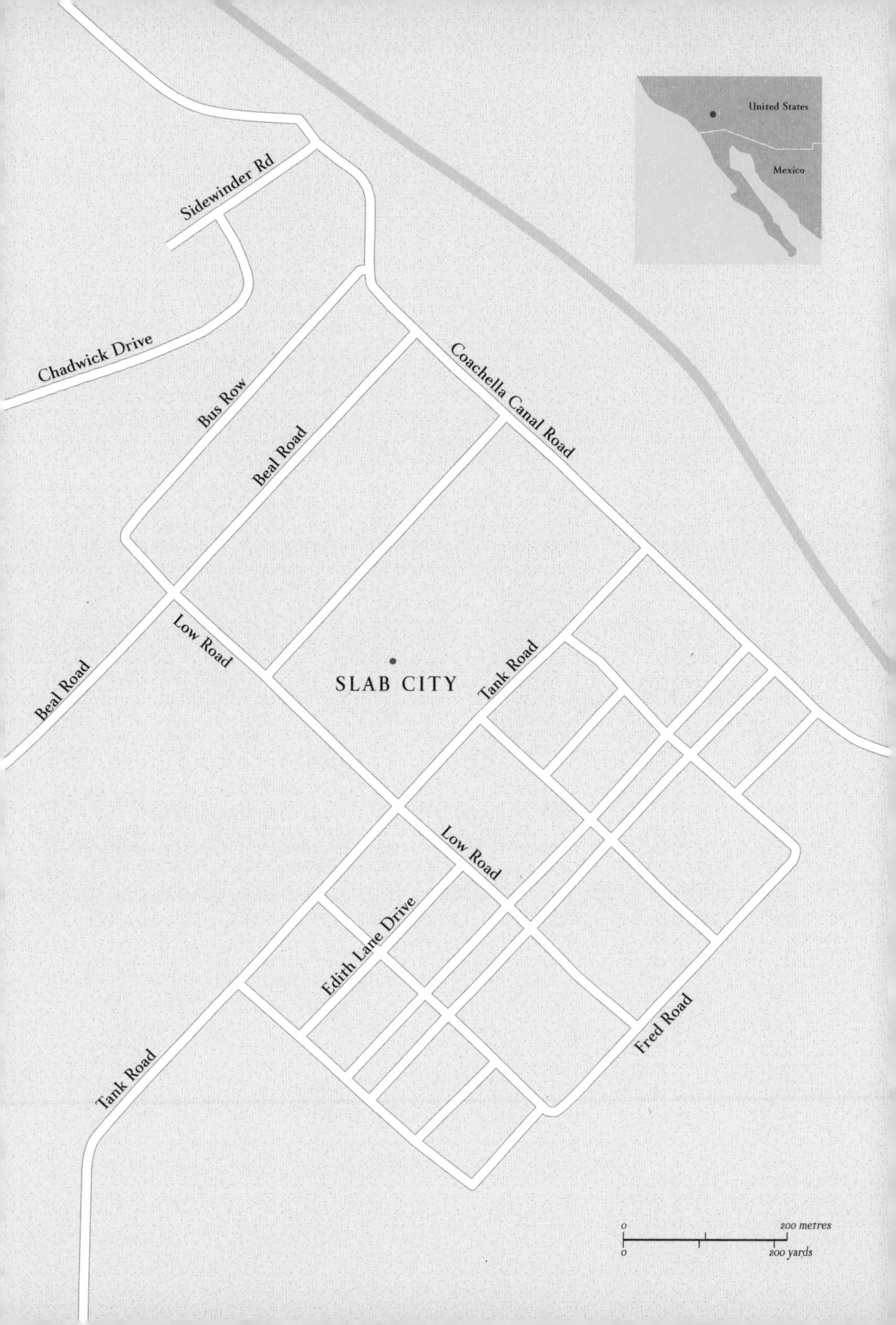

United States

Mexico

Sidewinder Rd

Chadwick Drive

Bus Row

Beal Road

Coachella Canal Road

Low Road

Beal Road

SLAB CITY

Tank Road

Low Road

Edith Lane Drive

Tank Road

Fred Road

| 0 | | 200 metres |
| 0 | | 200 yards |

accent is post-apocalyptic, or as *Time* magazine once put it, very 'Mad Max'. There is, however, a church, a library, community swap meetings for goods and services, and plenty of public art – including a sculpture park boasting a giant mammoth made out of used tyres, and an outdoor music venue, The Range, where concerts are staged each Saturday and a prom night held annually.

Run on a 'live and let live' basis, Slab City has for decades attracted, in equal measure, libertarians, the lost, the destitute, artists, the addled and addicted, hobos and eccentrics. In the fallout from the 2008 financial crash, though, families of 'recession refugees', relatively ordinary folk whose homes had been foreclosed or whose businesses failed, turned to Slab City as a last resort. Most stayed for a just a few weeks or months, using it as a stopgap to shore up their finances before plunging back into the 'real world' of jobs, running water, functioning sewers, refuse collection and electricity, but others valued living cheaply and without accruing further debts and have put down roots.

With temperature reaching as high as 120°F (48°C) in the summer, scorpions and rattlesnakes a constant presence on a ground strewn with military waste, and the nearest grocery store and post office in Niland, five miles away, it's perhaps not everyone's idea of paradise. And living law-lite and this far off-grid can have its less than savoury side. From meth labs to murders, Slab City sees its fair share of crime but perhaps no more proportionally than certain other American cities whose roads are paved and patrolled by armed officers. The state of California, however, may be on the cusp of intruding more formally on life in Slab City. Since the spring of 2015 it has been investigating the option of selling the land, and not for the first time. Up to this point, the additional costs of decontaminating the site have previously dissuaded potential purchasers. But with takers looking rather thicker on the ground this time round, the Slabbers have been forced to consider embarking on a community bid themselves. An outcome that will, according to some, inevitably spell the end for Slab City as a place open to all, free from rules and rents.

Left: Outsider art in excelsis at Slab City.

PORTMEIRION

THE VILLAGE

WALES [UNITED KINGDOM]

52° 54' 52" N
4° 5' 50" W

It seems wholly characteristic of Portmeirion and its progenitor, the gentleman/amateur architect Clough Williams-Ellis, that an eighteenth-century Ionic colonnade was accidentally mislaid under a compost heap for thirty years. It's not that Williams-Ellis was especially forgetful or careless with his estate, but it's easy to imagine how the odd bit of stonework might go astray while assembling this exuberantly fantastical place from the sheer profusion of architectural stuff – the gazebo, the bandstand, the campanile, archways, terraces, steps, obelisks, statues, trompe l'oeil effects and a full-scale ship modelled in concrete – lined up elsewhere.

Called 'the last folly of the Western world' and 'a giant gnomes' village', Portmeirion was Williams-Ellis's attempt to bring a touch of Portofino to North Wales. This in itself was a bold enough venture. Few believed that an ersatz Italianate-style village would sit easily on a corner of a craggy estuary off Cardigan Bay, but perhaps it was all the more successful for enjoying about the same relationship to a real Genoese fishing port as Pinocchio to the truth. It also benefits from being located on a Gulf Stream that allows a fine collection of subtropical plants to thrive. Their presence, along with a hodgepodge of buildings, ancient and modern, and many painted in bright pink and pale blues and yellows, only adds to its convincingly Mediterranean ambience.

The first purpose-built holiday resort in Britain, Portmeirion opened in 1926. And if anticipating the age of mass tourism, it simultaneously also summoned up the ghosts of the Grand Tour. Laid out not unlike an elaborate stage set, it was an instant hit with theatre and film people.

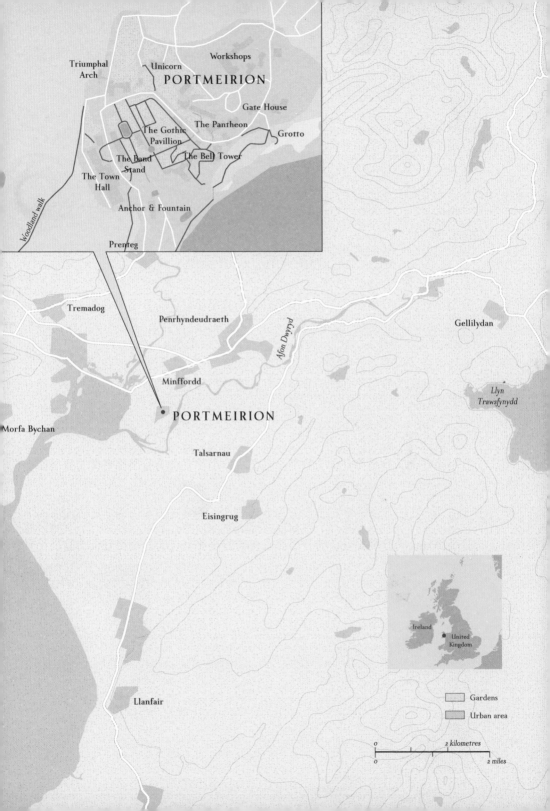

Triumphal
Arch

Unicorn

Workshops

PORTMEIRION

Gate House

The Pantheon

The Gothic
Pavillion

Grotto

The Band
Stand

The Bell Tower

The Town
Hall

Woodland walk

Anchor & Fountain

Prenteg

Tremadog

Penrhyndeudraeth

Gellilydan

Afon Dwyryd

Minffordd

Morfa Bychan

Llyn
Trawsfynydd

PORTMEIRION

Talsarnau

Eisingrug

Ireland

United
Kingdom

Llanfair

☐ Gardens

■ Urban area

0   2 kilometres

0   2 miles

Noël Coward, Larry Adler and Ingrid Bergman all holidayed here, along with the philosopher Bertrand Russell and King Zog of Albania. Coward, in fact, was to pen one of his most popular plays, *Blithe Spirit*, during a week-long stint at Portmeirion in 1941. The resort was to become famous the world over after it appeared as 'The Village' in the cult 1960s television series *The Prisoner*, staring Patrick McGoohan.

But Portmeirion's founding principle was always really to embody Clough Williams-Ellis himself.

A member of the Anglo-Welsh gentry, he was known for his impeccably eccentric dress, and usually wore knee-high yellow socks combined with breeches. A First World War veteran and a pioneering conservationist, Williams-Ellis completed only a single term as an architectural student and readily confessed to breaking into his chosen field via some 'family jobbery'. His list of clients included the former British Prime Minister David Lloyd George and the post-war new town of Stevenage, though an offer to move to Soviet Russia and work for Joseph Stalin was politely declined. Portmeirion was, however, the pride and joy of his life. It provided him with the chance to fulfil a dream 'to erect', as he once explained, 'a whole group of buildings on my chosen site for my own satisfaction; an ensemble that would indeed *be* me'.

Williams-Ellis, who lived to the ripe old age of ninety-four and was knighted just four years earlier, died in 1978. But Portmeirion, which has since survived both the vagaries of the tourist trade and a fire that destroyed the hotel's Cockpit Bar fashioned from the timbers of HMS *Arethusa* (a Napoleonic era man-of-war), stands as a lasting monument to a man who passionately believed that architecture's only virtue was in providing 'more fun for more people'.

Right: Portofino as conjured up in North Wales by Williams-Ellis.

Zvyozdny Gorodok

Star City [Russia]

55° 52' 41"N
38° 6' 44.7"E

It is the isolation, returning astronauts say, that is one of the most difficult things about journeying into space. Trapped in a tin can, floating hundreds of miles from home and performing monotonous tasks in monotonous situations with the same crew members for days, weeks, months and sometimes years on end – all this means that those boldly going where very few men, and even fewer women, have gone before experience mental pressures that always were, and will remain, intense.

The ability of space to mess with the minds of those venturing into it has long been understood. Astronauts aboard the early Apollo missions reported experiencing wild hallucinations, and at least one tour of duty on the Soviet Salyut 5 space station in the mid-1970s is widely understood to have been terminated prematurely after its crew suffered some kind of collective nervous breakdown. With potential voyages to Mars in the offing, both the European Space Agency and NASA have, in recent years, conducted extensive research trials in Antarctica and Hawaii to test the ability of human beings to endure lengthy solar system-spanning odysseys in the future. Using in some instances real spacecraft in these isolated locations, they've attempted to simulate the conditions of life on Mars or the experience of travelling to it and beyond.

But examine the history of manned space flight, and it seems that a particular sort of otherworldliness has been built in at the start. The Soviet Union's space programme, especially, though not exclusively, was shrouded in secrecy from its inception. In an ideological race to the stars, and the moon, mum really was the word in Mother Russia, and it was exemplified

Zvyozdny
Gorodok

Zvyozdny Gorodok
government buildings

STAR
CITY

Russia

Belarus

Ukraine

alovskoye sh.

Rail track

S Tsioikovskaya station

Cosmonaut training centre

Urban areas

0   500 metres

0   500 yards

by Zvyozdny Gorodok, or Star City, in Moscow Oblast, an outer borough north-west of the Soviet capital.

Officially known for a time simply as 'closed military townlet No. 1', its existence was a closely guarded secret, and one maintained by a substantial army presence. Living in a socially isolated bubble even before being blasted into the confines of outer space, cosmonauts ate, slept and breathed interstellar activity here. It evolved into the Yuri Gagarin Cosmonaut Training Centre in the 1960s – named in tribute to the first man in space, who also prepared for his epoch-making mission at Star City. Surviving the collapse of the Soviet Union, Star City, as it was formally renamed in the 1990s, remains a protected zone but it now has a museum of space travel open to the public.

Over the last two decades it has also worked collaboratively with NASA. Its Director of NASA Operations there between 2001 and 2003 was the Canadian astronaut Chris Hadfield. Hadfield's performance aboard the International Space Station of David Bowie's 'Space Oddity', a song about an alienated rocket man who abandons himself to the cosmos, became an internet sensation in 2013. In a subsequent memoir Hadfield recalled the collegiate atmosphere of Star City and one rather odd team-building exercise. For luck prior to blast-off, and in homage to Gagarin, who had to take an impromptu bathroom break en route to the launch pad on his groundbreaking voyage, crew members all urinate on the back rear tyre of the bus ferrying them to their space craft.

Right: Top flight facilities at Star City. Pictured here the training pool for cosmonauts.

Hearst Castle

Randolph Hearst's Xanadu-esque home

San Simeon, California [United States]

35° 41' 6"N
121° 10' 5"W

It is always intriguing to think about how and where we might live if money really were no object. With untold riches at our disposal, what sort of house would we choose? Few of us will ever have to worry about this, however. Having a roof over our heads at all is enough of a concern, but if we were to picture a place fit for a tycoon or a wealthy media mogul with more money than they knew what do with, odds on it probably wouldn't look too dissimilar to San Simeon.

Set on a rocky knoll, La Cuesta Encantada (or The Enchanted Hill) in the Santa Lucia Mountains, five miles and 1,600 feet above the San Simeon Bay in northern California, San Simeon (or Hearst Castle as it's popularly known) was the opulent retreat of the twentieth-century newspaper baron William Randolph Hearst.

A large, softy spoken man, fluent in French and German, and inclined to loud hand-painted ties and brightly coloured suits, Hearst has been all but eclipsed by his cinematic representation – Orson Welles's immortal caricature Charles Foster Kane in *Citizen Kane*. But the truth was odd enough without the shattered snow globes and seamless through-the-nightclub-roof tracking shots, and San Simeon, the model for Kane's Xanadu, easily exceeds its onscreen imitator.

Created over the course of twenty-eight years with the San Francisco-born architect Julia Morgan, the first woman ever permitted to study architecture at the Ecole des Beaux Arts, Paris, San Simeon was built to Hearst's exacting demands and to display his extraordinary collection of Old Masters, antiques, ancient artefacts, classical statues and even complete

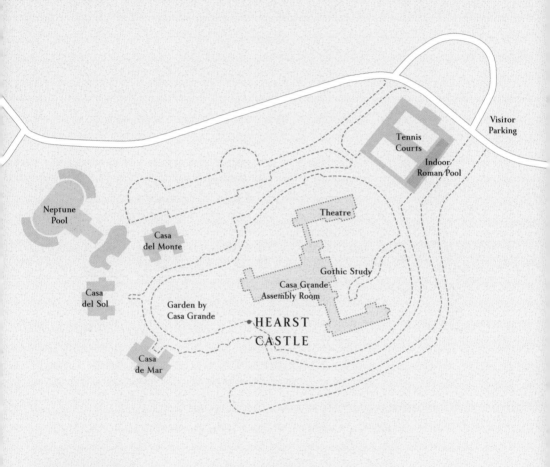

Neptune
Pool

Casa
del Monte

Casa
del Sol

Garden by
Casa Grande

Casa
de Mar

Tennis
Courts

Indoor
Roman Pool

Visitor
Parking

Theatre

Gothic Study

Casa Grande
Assembly Room

HEARST
CASTLE

USA

Mexico

- - - - Paved area

Out buildings

Hearst castle

0   20 metres

0   20 yards

buildings and their contents. An inveterate, intemperate hoover-upper of old stuff, Hearst at one point acquired a five-storey warehouse in the Bronx and filled it with his surplus purchases.

Though never completed and, in fact, left for good by its owner in 1947, San Simeon grew to encompass a complex of guest houses and a Mediterranean-style grand palace with an overall total of 165 rooms, 41 fireplaces and 61 bathrooms, along with a tennis court, stables, a private zoo and an 81-foot-long Roman pool with gold tiles. All this ranges over 127 acres, Hearst calling it, with epic understatement, 'my little hideaway'.

One of the many distinguished guests – there was rarely any other kind at San Simeon – was the British comic novelist P.G. Wodehouse. Employed as a scriptwriter for a Hollywood studio, Wodehouse left a vivid description of the place at its Hearst-ian zenith.

'The ranch', Wodehouse wrote in a letter in February 1931, 'is about half-way between Hollywood and San Francisco. It is on the top of a high hill, and just inside the entrance gates is a great pile of stones, which, if you ever put them together, would form an old abbey which Hearst bought in France and shipped over and didn't know what to do with so left lying by the wayside. The next thing you see, having driven past this, is a yak or a buffalo or something in the middle of the road. Hearst collects animals and has a zoo on the premises, and the ones considered reasonably harmless are allowed to roam at large. You're apt to meet a bear or two before you get to the house. The house is enormous, and there are always at least fifty guests staying there. All the furniture is period, and you probably sleep on a bed originally occupied by Napoleon or somebody.'

As a ten-year-old, Hearst had accompanied his mother, Phoebe, a former schoolteacher, on an eighteen-month tour of Europe – the pair visiting every significant museum, gallery, ruin, castle and church in Ireland, Scotland, England, France, Italy, Switzerland, Austria, Germany, Belgium and Holland, and dining with American consuls, and meeting the Pope in Rome, along the way. And it's impossible not to see much of Hearst's adult life as an elaborate attempt to recreate the highlights of that tour from a jumble of consoling pre-pubescent memories. Winston Churchill, another Hearst house guest and one who 'got to like him', summed him up as 'a grave simple child – with no doubt a nasty temper – playing with the most costly toys'.

But as Hearst was to discover, even his finances were not inexhaustible. Hit by a stock market crash and economic depression that followed it, he was forced to sell several of his businesses. With his health also failing, he moved to a more modest abode in Beverly Hills and died a much-reduced

Above: San Simeon, Hearst's 'little hideaway', viewed from the air. The 'casas' house an incredible sixty bathrooms.

figure of influence in 1951. Incorporated into a state park, San Simeon has been open as a public museum and zoo since 1958, though Hearst's descendants still live in parts of the property at certain times of the year.

DESERTED DESTINATIONS

Teufelsberg

Abandoned U.S. spy station

Berlin [Germany]

52° 29' 49" N
13° 14' 27" E

At the far west of the German capital, Berlin, there is a green oasis, the forest of Grunewald, whose trees and lakes stretch down to meet the sandy eastern bank and pellucid waters of the River Havel. Before the Second World War, the neighbouring quarter, which remains affluent, was favoured for its leafiness as a place of residence by the wealthy, though given short shrift by the novelist Christopher Isherwood. In 1920, the author of *Goodbye to Berlin* described the Grunewald as a 'dank, dreary pinewood' and maintained that the district's palatial villas were built in 'all known styles of expensive ugliness'. The forest was also intended to provide the suitably Teutonic setting for an elite Nazi *Wehrtechnische Fakultät*, or military technical training school. To a blueprint by Hitler's chief architect Albert Speer to resemble the kind of medieval castle that angry peasants in black-and-white horror movies approach with pitchforks and flaming torches, its construction started in 1937 but faltered in 1940 and was never completed.

Four years after the war, in 1949, Berlin was carved in two by the victorious, if now ideologically divided, Allied powers – into West Berlin, composed of sectors administered by the Americans, British and French but officially part of West Germany, and East Berlin under Soviet Russia and the capital of communist East Germany. The Grunewald fell under West Berlin. But for more than forty years that entire half of the city was an island completely surrounded by East Germany. Its sense of separateness was only further underscored by the construction in 1961 of the Berlin Wall. In places 13 feet high, this ring of brick, concrete and barbed wire

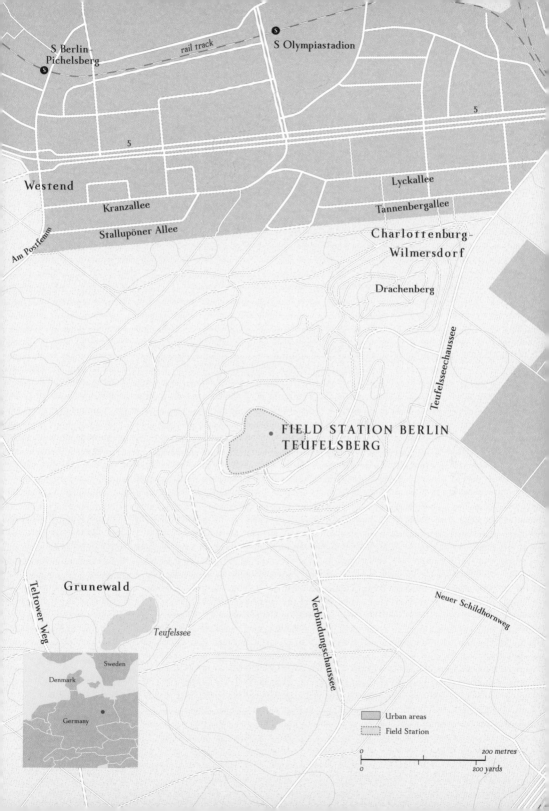

S Berlin-
Pichelsberg

rail track

S Olympiastadion

5

Westend

Kranzallee

Lyckallee

Tannenbergallee

Stallupöner Allee

Charlottenburg-
Wilmersdorf

Am Postfenn

Drachenberg

Teufelsseechaussee

FIELD STATION BERLIN
TEUFELSBERG

Grunewald

Teltower Weg

Teufelssee

Neuer Schildhornweg

Verbindungschaussee

Sweden

Denmark

Germany

Urban areas

Field Station

0   200 metres

0   200 yards

cordoned off the west from the east, and was put up, according to the East German government, to act as an 'anti-fascist protection barrier'.

If the Wall largely prevented East Germans fleeing to the west, it also added to West Berliners' sense of isolation from the outlying countryside; a countryside they could only journey through on four designated transit roads, not stopping until they reached the main border of West Germany. Unsurprisingly, the Grunewald, as one of the wildest, and the largest, green spaces in West Berlin, was much cherished by the city residents as a resort for nature rambles and picnics during the Cold War era.

The most striking feature of the forest is a large scrubby hill that stands 377 feet above sea level and is the highest elevation in this flat and low-lying, low-rise metropolis. History is often said to be written into the landscape, like a palimpsest. Here that is truer than usual, for the hill, known as Devil's Mountain (Teufelsberg) and nicknamed Mount Junk (der Monte Klamotte), was formed from the blasted rubble of old Berlin. Simply unable to shift the wreckage from Allied bombing beyond the limits of the newly divided city, West Berlin, out of expediency as much as anything, opted to shift it into the comparatively open ground of the forest. Around 635.6 million cubic feet of architectural detritus, from marble balustrades to iron staircases, were ferried here and actually piled up on top of Speer's unfinished *Wehrtechnische Fakultät*. The city's recent, and by association, shameful past was quite literally buried, a process that continued as the tainted remnants of yesteryear were torn down in a post-war rebuilding programme that understandably fetishized the new and the modern as the healthiest means of moving on. Accordingly the Devil's Mountain was made over into a winter sports facility with a ski jump, ski lifts and a toboggan run, the latter enjoyed by Berliners to this day. But the erection of the Wall led to other features being added to this already unorthodox edifice and they included a search tower and a British-American signal monitoring complex.

The peak of Teufelsberg, with its unimpeded views of all Berlin beneath it, was the ideal location to site powerful receivers for British and American intelligence to eavesdrop on the Eastern bloc. The ski lifts seemingly interfered with the equipment and were removed but a fairground Ferris wheel in nearby Zehlendorf was somehow discovered to enhance reception and so it was left *in situ*.

The architecture of the complex itself was scarcely less fantastical: its most arresting element by the early 1970s was a trio of white geodesic domes that would have looked equally at home on the moon or on Luke Skywalker's Tatooine. In the mid-1980s the radio signal station was enlarged and conditions for staff improved with the addition of a gym, a casino and even a *Biergarten*.

But, with the fall of the Wall in 1989 and the reunification of Germany, Teufelsberg soon became surplus to Anglo-American spying requirements and was closed in 1991. It was subsequently sold to a private investment company, though plans to redevelop it into apartments and, more intriguingly, a yoga and meditation centre backed by the American film director David Lynch, have come and gone. In the intervening years the station deteriorated physically, its once gleaming facilities broken, rusted and covered in the graffiti which in Berlin is daubed on city buildings almost as an act of public duty, and left out of civic pride. And while its long-term future is unknown, the site is at the time of writing leased to a firm which conducts regular guided tours and events, where the curious can hear all about a place formerly devoted to listening in on other people's conversations.

Below: Eavesdropping on the East – Teufelsberg at the height of the Cold War.

PRESIDIO MODELO

CUBA'S MOST NOTORIOUS FORMER PENITENTIARY

ISLA DE LA JUVENTUD [CUBA]

21° 46' 52"N
79° 57' 15"W

'Panopticon', from the Greek παν- ('all') and -οπτικος ('seeing'), is a house of incarceration where the inmates are to be kept under constant surveillance by their gaolers. The British philosopher and prision reformer Jeremy Bentham first conceived this new type of prison in the 1780s after being inspired by an observation platform at Prince Potemkin's estate in Russia which allowed foremen to direct gangs of peasant workers. The system Bentham imagined would be both efficient to run, requiring fewer staff, and, he believed, improve the behaviour of jailbirds into the bargain, leading them to emerge reformed at their end of their terms. Though it attracted the interest of the British government and the architect Willey Reveley was commissioned to draw up a plan for a building in 1791, Bentham's hopes of erecting his own 'panopticon' on a site beside the Thames in London, now occupied by Tate Britain, eventually came to nothing. But the concept outlived its creator and has ever since shaped the design of prisons – and much else besides.

One of the finest examples – however thorny an issue the use of that adjective may be in this context – of a panopticon prison was Presidio Modelo, itself modelled on the notoriously unforgiving Stateville Correctional Center in Crest Hill, Illinois, USA.

Presidio Modelo was inaugurated in 1926 on what was then called the Isla de Pinos – or Isle of Pines – off the southwestern coast of Cuba by Gerardo Machado y Morales, the country's democratically elected president turned repressive dictator. Completed a few years later, Presidio Modelo was composed of four six-storey circular blocks, each overlooked

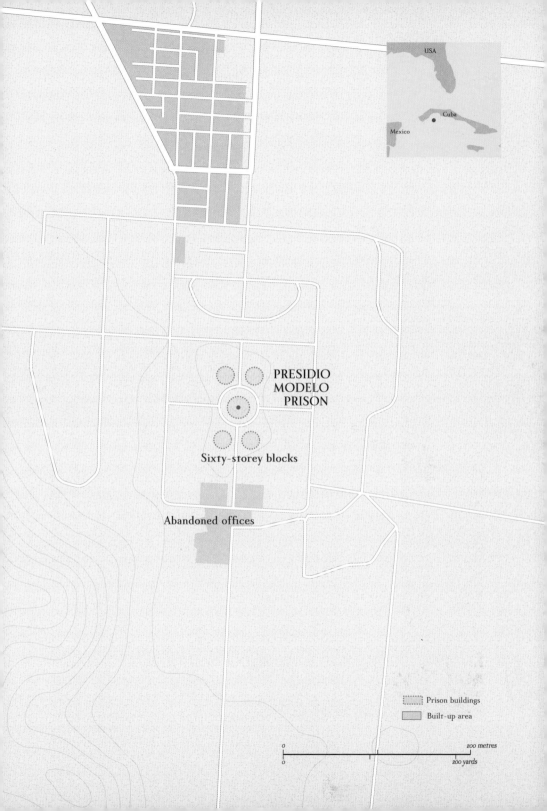

USA

Cuba

Mexico

PRESIDIO
MODELO
PRISON

Sixty-storey blocks

Abandoned offices

Prison buildings

Built-up area

0   200 metres
0   200 yards

by a central watchtower, and the facility was capable of housing up to 6,000 prisoners.

Two of its most famous internees were the future Cuban leaders Fidel and Raúl Castro, who were held there after their attempted revolt against the Moncada Barracks in Santiago in 1953. Six years later, the revolutionary Fidel Castro, triumphant over the American-supported

Below: The Presidio Modelo 'panopticon' prison, home for a time to the future Cuban leaders Fidel and Raúl Castro.

government of Fulgencio Batista, who had himself helped lead the overthrow of Machado, began using the same prison to house his own political opponents. But after episodes of severe overcrowding, hunger strikes and riots, Presidio Modelo was closed in 1967. Since designated as a national monument, this 'panopticon' has, ironically, become an object of interest to sightseers.

Battleship Island

Deserted mining settlement

Hashima, Nagasaki [Japan]

32° 37' 40.2"N
129° 44' 18.9"E

Villains in James Bond films tend to have not homes but lairs, much as they have henchmen (and women) rather than employees with contracts, remuneration packages and pension schemes. These lairs are usually in exotic and out-of-the-way locations – the top of a snow-capped Alpine mountain, inside the shell of a spent volcano, underwater or out in the dark recesses of space generally seem to have had the edge over the uptown neighbourhood or commutable suburb for the likes of Goldfinger, Blofeld, Stromberg and Drax. It's mostly a question of space: where, when it comes down to it, does one house an arsenal of deadly weapons, teams of crack scientists, harems of lithe young women with martial arts skills and platoons of anonymous grunts? Interrelatedly, the need to hatch diabolical world-dominating schemes safe from the prying eyes of the security services has led many a Bond foe to opt for a distant island retreat. Raoul Silva, the former MI6 agent turned vengeful cyberterrorist, in 2012's *Skyfall*, the twenty-third official James Bond film, certainly followed in this noble (or, perhaps, ignoble) tradition, one firmly established in the Bond movie-going public's imagination by such earlier island-dwelling super-crooks as Dr No and Francisco Scaramanga.

In *Skyfall*, Silva, the sporter of a prosthetic jaw, left hideously scarred physically and mentally by imprisonment and torture by the Chinese, occupies a decayed island city somewhere off the coast of Macau. Falsely rumoured to be contaminated by a chemical leak, this isolated property is covered with deliquescing concrete blocks like jagged teeth and piles of rubble and rusting machinery. Its appearance mirrors perfectly the insane,

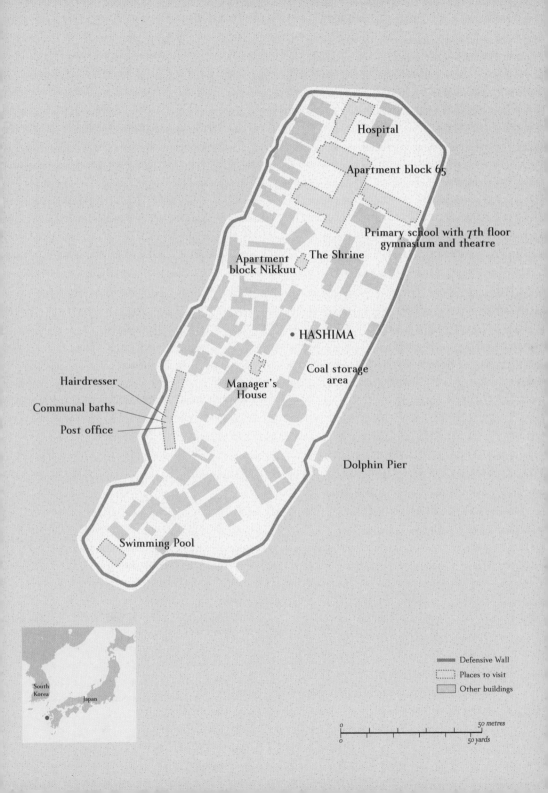

Hospital

Apartment block 65

Primary school with 7th floor
gymnasium and theatre

Apartment
block Nikkuu

The Shrine

• HASHIMA

Coal storage
area

Hairdresser

Manager's
House

Communal baths

Post office

Dolphin Pier

Swimming Pool

South
Korea

Japan

Defensive Wall

Places to visit

Other buildings

0   50 metres

0   50 yards

web-savvy criminal's twisted character. As a backdrop to fictional acts of evil intent, it is easily one of the most arresting and truly sinister-looking of any of the Bond villain lairs committed to celluloid. More unbelievably perhaps, Silva's island is a real place – though by all accounts studio replicas aided and abetted the bulk of its appearances on screen.

Officially its name is Hashima. But this isle about nine miles out from the southern Japanese coast near Nagasaki in the East China Sea is more commonly known as Gunkanjima (or Battleship Island) in tribute to the fearsome silhouette its rotted buildings cast on the horizon. This lonely and typhoon-beaten rock was left entirely to its own devices until coal was discovered beneath its seabed in the 1880s. Then the Japanese industrial giant Mitsubishi set up a mining operation there. At first miners were ferried across from the mainland, but soon the company began building accommodation on the island itself. In 1916 Japan's first ever concrete high-rise block was erected here, and its slim rain-lashed and windswept 16-acre surface was to become one of the most densely populated places on earth, with more than 5,000 men, women and children cooped up on Hashima at its peak. The mine closed in 1974 and with it also went the people, who abandoned the island in a heartbeat, leaving their furnished apartments and offices, a cinema, a supermarket, a gymnasium, a school and a medical centre to the elements. Forty-something years on, Hashima appears feral and haunted, its streets strewn with detritus and its mottled and pockmarked modernist housing standing like towering jack-o'-lanterns with their cracked fascias and hollow, empty windows.

All places have their ghosts and Hashima's history is anything but rosy. However, since 2015 the deserted 'ship' has been listed as a World Heritage Site by UNESCO, this floating rock standing as a somewhat ravaged symbol of Japan's transformation into an industrial nation.

Left: Crumbling concrete apartment blocks on Hashima. The abandoned island was home to Japan's first high-rise tower.

NO MAN'S LAND FORT

A LONG SHUNNED COASTAL BULWARK

THE SOLENT [UNITED KINGDOM]

50° 44' 22" N
1° 5' 41" W

The poet John Donne said no man is an island, but No Man's Land Fort is an island of sorts. One of four iron and granite structures, it is set like tarnished stones in the murky tidal waters of the Solent, a mile or so off the south coast of England. As perfect examples of robust, self-confident, enduring Victorian engineering as you could possibly find, they nevertheless speak volumes of the geopolitical anxieties of that age. Like Spitbank, Horse Sand and St Helens, No Man's Land Fort was erected between 1860 and 1880 in direct response to very real fears of a potential threat of invasion from across the English Channel. In 1860, the British Prime Minister, Lord Palmerston, established a Royal Commission on the Defence of the United Kingdom, which recommended a substantial expansion of coastal bulwarks to protect naval ports such as Portsmouth. Squabbles over their cost would delay their completion and by the time No Man's Land was finally up and operating it was largely irrelevant. Both it and similar forts were popularly dismissed as 'Palmerston's Follies'.

Below: No Man's Land Fort, the first line of defence against a potential invasion.

However, the First and Second World Wars were to dent such naysaying attitudes, as they were re-armed and manned as vital coastal defences. Decommissioned in the 1950s, No Man's Land sat for years largely in a state of abeyance. Since 2008, it has since been revamped as a luxury hotel and party venue, with a helipad, a wine bar, billiard room, swimming pool, laser quest arena and guest rooms, most decorated in a nautical theme, with portraits of Lord Nelson a charming addition to some.

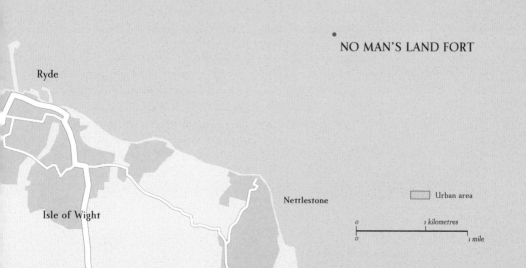

Portsmouth
Harbour

Portsmouth

Ireland

United
Kingdom

Gosport

Southsea

Spitsand Fort

SOLENT

Horse Sand Fort

NO MAN'S LAND FORT

Ryde

Nettlestone

Urban area

Isle of Wight

0   1 kilometres

0   1 mile

The Lost City of San Juan Parangaricutiro

Abandoned after the eruption of 1943

Mexico [Central America]

19° 37' 4" N
102° 17' 8" w

Overleaf: The tower and remaining bodice of the Church of San Juan Parangaricutiro, the only survivor of a town destroyed by the lava flow of Paricutin Volcano.

O n 20 February 1943, the residents of the Mexican town of San Juan Parangaricutiro awoke to the sound of church bells ringing. Not an especially unusual occurrence in this part of the world, you might think. On this occasion, however, the bells appeared to be ringing of their own volition. Their chimes were also accompanied by something rather more ominous: the distant, low rumble of the earth shaking. Two miles away the Parícutin volcano had erupted and was beginning to spout molten lava.

Fortunately, only a handful of people were harmed in the eruption itself and the flow of the lava was extremely slow. It would be a year before it eventually reached the town, allowing everyone plenty of time to pack up and leave. If snail-paced, the lava nevertheless consumed virtually everything in its path, leaving thousands homeless and jobless and destroying crops and farmland. Over the course of the next eight years it gradually blanketed the entire town in a thick layer of volcanic rock, swallowing up whole streets of houses and even flowing indiscriminately over tombstones in the church graveyard. But when its destructive course finally came to an end, one lone building was left partially intact. Miraculously, the local church emerged largely unscathed. Its great bell tower and the altar were spared entirely and stand to this day marooned in a grim expanse of solidified lava.

Believed by some to symbolize God's grace, the church has become a site of pilgrimage. All that remains of the original San Juan Parangaricutiro, it appears in the landscape as if holding a lonely vigil for the lost community it once served, its endurance only helping further to emphasize the awesome destructive power of nature.

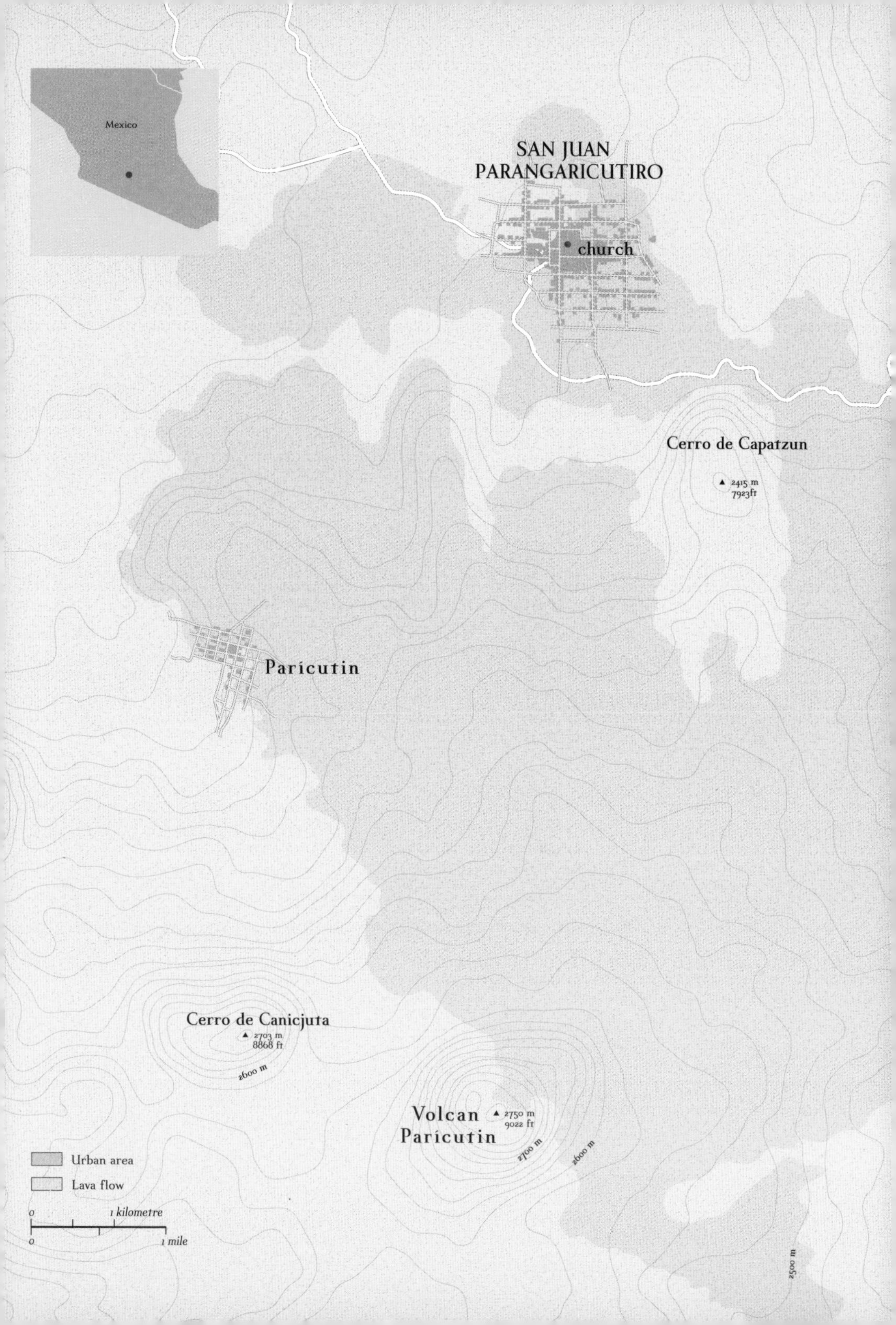

Mexico

SAN JUAN
PARANGARICUTIRO

church

Cerro de Capatzun

▲ 2415 m
7923 ft

Parícutin

Cerro de Canicjuta

▲ 2703 m
8868 ft

2600 m

Volcan
Parícutin

▲ 2750 m
9022 ft

2700 m

2600 m

2500 m

Urban area

Lava flow

0   1 kilometre

0   1 mile

Humberstone and Santa Laura

Redundant saltpetre works

Humberstone [Chile]

27° 22' 50"N
70° 19' 59"E

Saltpetre, or potassium nitrate, is the major component of gunpowder. But if it can help blow things up it was also once used in fertilizers to grow plants and crops, and the place gifted with the largest deposits on earth of this life-giving (and -taking) substance was the Atacama Desert, the driest non-polar desert on the planet, which stretches from southern Peru into northern Chile. The presence in this region of what became an increasingly valuable resource led to Chile fighting the War of the Pacific with Peru and Bolivia in 1880s. This conflict (sometimes dubbed the Nitrate War) lasted four years and cost the lives of thousands, but Chile emerged victorious, having successfully annexed some of the richest saltpetre territories of its South American neighbours. It was to become the biggest single supplier of natural saltpetre in the world, with the use of nitrate fertilizers ushering in a global revolution in agriculture. Complicit in all this were the British, who had substantial involvement and financial interests in Chilean saltpetre production and an expanding population at home and across its empire to feed.

The town of Humberstone, then known as La Palma, was first founded around a nitrate mine in 1862. It was renamed in 1925 in honour of its enterprising former manager James Humberstone, a British chemical engineer and entrepreneur. Humberstone had arrived in what was then still part of Peru as an energetic and ambitious twenty-five-year-old employee of the Tarapacá Nitrate Company in 1873. Within a couple of years he had succeeded in doubling the efficiency of the company's plants, a feat he achieved by introducing a new process for refining the local white *caliche*,

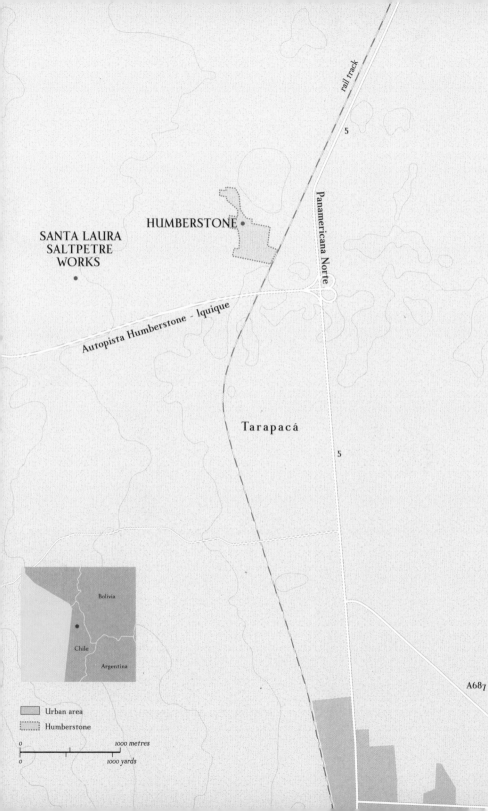

rail track

5

HUMBERSTONE

SANTA LAURA
SALTPETRE
WORKS

Panamericana Norte

Autopista Humberstone - Iquique

Tarapacá

5

Bolivia

Chile

Argentina

A68₁

Urban area
Humberstone

| 0 | | | 1000 metres |
| 0 | | | 1000 yards |

one initially developed by the Lancashire firm of Shanks for separating sodium carbonate from black ash. It was the first of many innovations of Humberstone's lengthy career. Known as 'Don Santiago' and crowned 'the Father of the Nitrate Industry', he died in 1939, having received an Order of the British Empire from King Edward VIII, and was buried in the Cementerio de los Ingleses (British Cemetery) at Hacienda Tilviche. By that time the town bearing his name, and its nearby sister Salitrera Santa Laura, were at their peak. The population of Humberstone was then some 3,700-strong and it was the undisputed centre of Chile's saltpetre production. Beside the mine and the works and houses, there were schools, a theatre in a smart modernist style where the Chilean folksinger Violeta Parra once played, a marketplace plaza, a company shop, a hotel where visiting industry executives stayed and were wined and dined, a ballroom and tennis courts. But the appearance now of mass-produced man-made nitrates, first synthesized in Germany shortly before the First World War, spelled doom for Humberstone and Santa Laura and its ilk. The factory at Humberstone was finally wound up in 1961, after nearly twenty years of what modern-day economists might call 'managed decline'.

The story goes that shortly after the last of the residents had left, both towns and the surrounding land were sold as a job lot to a dealer who planned to profit by stripping out the plant and selling everything on as scrap. Fortunately he went bankrupt before he could carry out his scheme. And if subject to the abrasions of the weather, petty vandalism and the pilfering of some of the choice bits of plant, these towns were nevertheless left ghostly and mostly untouched, and as early as 1970 recognized as national historic monuments to the heyday of Chile's nitrates boom. Preserved in situ at Santa Laura are the remains of an old railway line, piles of gas equipment, coolers, metal cutters and steel girders, much of it Victorian imports from Britain and bearing manufacturers' stamps from Yorkshire and Scotland. A monstrous-looking *planta de chancado*, or caliche crusher, maintains a silent vigil over the whole scene, a forlorn emblem of the works' decline. While there is a wealth of industrial relics including the town's old electrical power plant, Humberstone also houses a museum in the old company shop, and in the light of recent earthquakes preservation and restoration work has been stepped up on other buildings. A powerful sense of the loss of a whole way of life hangs over it all, like the omnipresent dust constantly blowing in from the desert. At the old municipal *piscina*, the cast-iron swimming pool is waterless, rusting and covered in graffiti, but the diving board remains intact, encouraging visitors to remember the work and play of a once prestigious industrial town.

Wonderland

ABANDONED DISNEYLAND-STYLE THEME PARK

NEAR BEIJING [CHINA]

40° 17' 5" N
116° 4' 41" E

If imitation is the sincerest form of flattery, such compliments seldom play too well with trademark holders. But where inspiration comes from, or where it goes, can sometimes be tricky to pin down. A bit of borrowing can go a long way in the creative arts and for culture as a whole. Take, for instance, Schloss Neuschwanstein, the fairytale castle that 'mad' King Ludwig II built for himself in the 1880s in southwestern Bavaria as a rural retreat. Modern-day visitors to Schloss Neuschwanstein are often struck by a nagging feeling that they've seen this uncanny turreted structure somewhere else. And usually they have. Or definitely something very much like it anyway, since the Bavarian monarch's architectural gimcrack is believed to have supplied Walt Disney with the model for the castle for his own Sleeping Beauty. The central structure of the first Disneyland amusement park, its image normally accompanied by a wand-waving Tinker Bell, is familiar to millions from its appearance in the animated opening sequence of Disney television shows and movies for more than sixty years.

But such castles haunted the human imagination before either Ludwig or Disney gave them their individual forms, and in both cases these men relied upon the inventiveness of theatrical set designers and artists alongside architects to realize their dream buildings. And our dreams, thankfully to date at least, are no respecters of copyright. Still, those arriving at Wonderland, or what was left of it until very recently, could have been forgiven for thinking they were suffering from déjà vu.

Storybook turrets and castellations were something of recurring motifs of the buildings at this amusement park 20 miles outside central

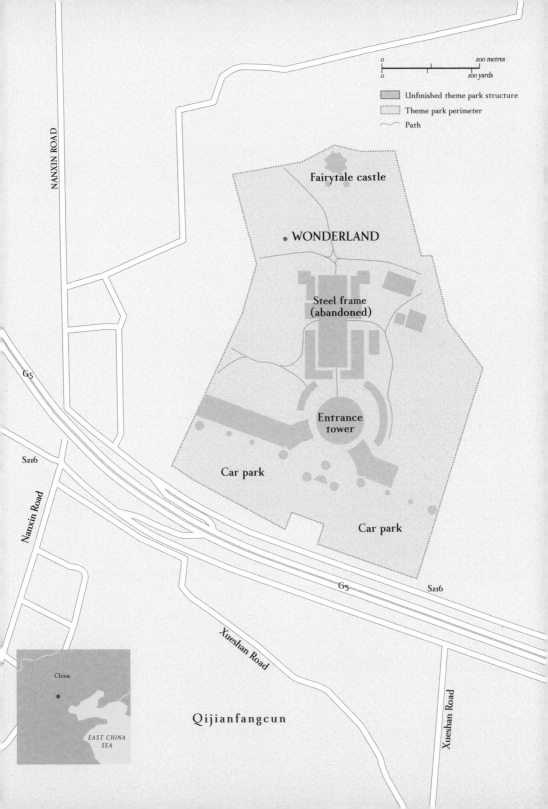

o   200 metres
o   200 yards

▢ Unfinished theme park structure
▢ Theme park perimeter
〰 Path

NANXIN ROAD

Fairytale castle

• WONDERLAND

Steel frame
(abandoned)

Entrance
tower

Car park

Car park

G5

S216

G5

S216

Nanxin Road

Xueshan Road

Xueshan Road

China

EAST CHINA
SEA

Qijianfangcun

Beijing. Promoting it as 'the largest amusement park in Asia', its developers confidently expected it to attract three million paying visitors a year. And out in Changping district on a former cornfield, a fantastical medieval landscape of citadels and mock keeps gradually arose, with a Neuschwansteinesque Schloss as its beating heart intended to tower above it all. As plainly artificial as it was Arthurian, Wonderland arguably had the makings of a place as fit for Tinker Bell as Ludwig. A cheery cartoon dragon posing by the Schloss was to be the park's logo, something that might also have won the approval of the Bavarian king – he was the patron of Wagner, whose *Ring Cycle* has no shortage of turns from these mythic beasts.

But construction on the site was halted in 1998 amid disputes over the land and the arrest of one of its main political backers on corruption charges. Attempts to secure other funds to revive the park in the run-up to the 2008 Beijing Olympic Games failed. Until the bulldozers moved in to level it in 2013, Wonderland's castles were crumbling away as if built of sand, their walls attracting only graffiti rather than tapestries and everything else around going to rack and ruin. Farmers banished from this magic kingdom had already begun to return, sowing crops inside empty buildings and claiming open plots where the developers envisaged car parks, turnstiles and ticket booths. In this, not only was reality reasserting itself over Wonderland's naive chimera but also, and in a neat inversion of the age of chivalry, the agrarian peasantry had come out on top for once.

Right: Wonderland's never-finished magic castle. The turret's a reminder of the once fairytale dream.

ORADOUR-SUR-GLANE

VILLAGE LEFT ABANDONED SINCE THE SECOND WORLD WAR

LIMOUSIN [FRANCE]

45° 55' 51" N
1° 1' 57" E

Limousin in central southern France is a region of ambling hills, lush meadows, clear lakes and verdant forests. Rural almost to a fault, it gives its name to a local breed of cattle, doe-eyed and russet brown, and a cloak worn by shepherds – the latter subsequently purloined to describe a type of car with a longer roof and bonnet, known universally for cresting up to red carpets. Its towns and villages, though, are bucolic, sleepy and full of character, with charming squares and no shortage of medieval churches, castles, arched stone bridges and turreted fifteenth-century chateaux either. All of which possibly reinforces the feeling that history has been an infrequent visitor to these parts since the Hundred Years War. Its very sense of isolation was certainly a draw to Impressionist painters such as Claude Monet, who frequently depicted its rural beauty.

But on a single day in 1944, one of its most unassuming settlements, Oradour-sur-Glane, a village with twelve cafés and which is some 15 miles north of the porcelain-producing metropolis of Limoges, was subjected to one of the worst atrocities committed on French soil in the twentieth century. For reasons that still cannot be explained or understood – or, perhaps more accurately, are indefensible – 646 people were murdered here by a unit of the Nazi 2nd SS Panzer Division, Das Reich.

This battle-weary German unit, only recently arrived in south-western France from the Eastern Front, was ordered north in the immediate wake of the D-Day landings. The prime targets were the French resistance, who were suspected, correctly, of being emboldened by recent gains by the Allies.

United Kingdom

France

Bellac

Gartempe River

280 m

300 m

360 m

400 m

400 m

La Couze

400 m

440 m
400 m
360 m

320 m

480 m 520 m

440 m

400 m

280 m

400 m

360 m

ORADOUR-
SUR-GLANE

Glane River

320 m

280 m

360 m

320 m

400 m

240 m

*Vienne
River*

320 m
280 m
240 m

200 m

280 m

240 m

Limoges

Urban area

Oradour-sur-Glane

0   3 *kilometres*

0   3 *miles*

The scale of this massacre – men, women, small children and small babies numbered among the dead – subsequently convinced General de Gaulle to order the village to be left exactly as it was upon its destruction in 1944. A new village would arise next door, but the old one continues to keep it company, the bleakest shadow imaginable for a cheery enough place of 2,000 residents now. In old Oradour-sur-Glane, the mayor's burnt-out

Below: A burnt-out car lying where it was parked in 1944.

Peugeot 202 sits exactly where it was parked more than seventy years ago, in a road grown mossy, and undisturbed by traffic ever since. Rusting Singer sewing machines and pots and pans, and meat hooks and a set of scales, lie in what little stands of former houses and shops. The village rests as a sobering memorial to the dead and as a resolute symbol of remembrance.

Muynak

Drained port
ARAL SEA [UZBEKISTAN]

43° 47' 2" N
59° 1' 30" E

Flounder, catfish and saltwater carp, the catches from the Aral Sea, were once so rich and plentiful that it alone provided a sixth of all the fish eaten across the entire USSR. Back then the fishermen of Muynak in Uzbekistan prided themselves on being the finest in the Soviet fleet. But Muynak no longer throngs with thousands of fisherfolk, nor does it even look out onto a vista of choppy waters. Instead it lies surrounded on all sides by bare expanses of loamy, salt-laced desert sand and is now some eighty miles from the sea. Fleets of once working trawlers have been left stranded and landlocked by the sea's receding waters. In what amounts to a ship's graveyard of oxidizing wrecks, rows of them are perched on top of bone-dry dunes; their hulls dusty and rusting, their propellers and rudders exposed, parched of water and looking pitiful and almost indecent somehow.

The retreat of the Aral Sea, around whose increasingly dry basin some sixty million people live, began after the Second World War. It was then that a scheme was devised to stoke cotton production in Uzbekistan and Turkmenistan. To do this, under what the Soviet Union called its 'Great Plan for the Transformation of Nature', two of the region's main rivers, the Amu Darya and the Syr Darya, were diverted to irrigate land for cotton fields. These reroutings, undertaken in the 1950s, had the desired effect: Uzbekistan ranks among the top ten cotton-producing nations in the world today. But a downside was a loss of water flowing to the Aral Sea. What was once the sea bed is now salty sand, prowled by wild camels safe in the knowledge that the tides of the Aral show no intention of returning.

Overleaf: The Aral Sea's retreat has created a boat cemetery on the salty sands of Muynak.

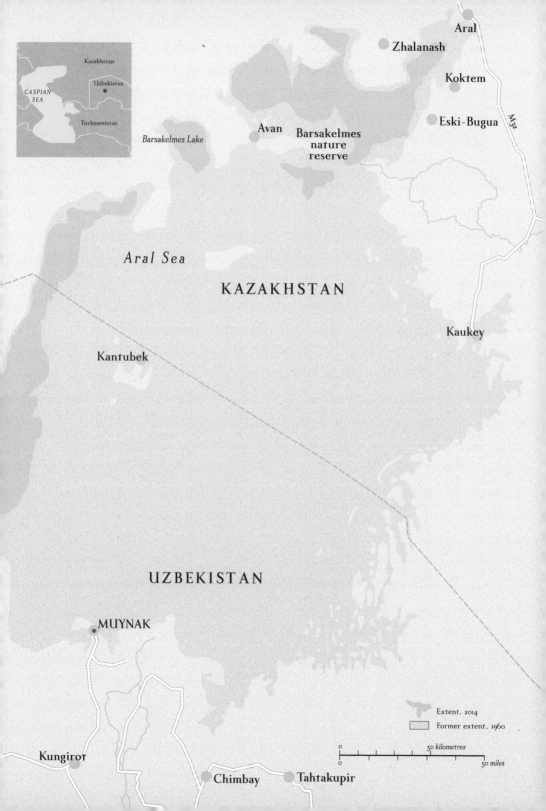

Kazakhstan

CASPIAN
SEA

Uzbekistan

Turkmenistan

Barsakelmes Lake

Aral

Zhalanash

Koktem

Eski-Bugua

M32

Avan

Barsakelmes
nature
reserve

Aral Sea

KAZAKHSTAN

Kaukey

Kantubek

UZBEKISTAN

MUYNAK

Kungirot

Chimbay

Tahtakupir

Extent, 2014

Former extent, 1960

0   50 kilometres

0   50 miles

WITTENOOM

ASBESTOS-RIDDEN INDUSTRIAL TOWN
WITTENOOM [WESTERN AUSTRALIA]

22° 14' 7" N
118° 20' 8" E

The Pilbara is a region in the north of the state of Western Australia. It's a landscape of rocky, russet mountain ranges, green gorges, wind-whipped deserts and icy cool lakes whose scenic beauty comes frequently in the extremes of its contrasts. The state is home to the magnificent Karijini National Park, one of this far-flung corner of Australia's most popular destinations. But this geologically ancient place is mining country. Its rocks and gorges are estimated to be 2,000 million years old and rich in minerals, and the deposits of one resource, once highly profitable, was to be the making, and the appalling breaking, of Wittenoom, a town whose residents were to suffer one of the worst tragedies of this young nation's recent history. The resource found here on the distant slopes of the Hamersley Range some 880 miles from Perth was crocidolite, or blue asbestos.

Known once as 'woolly stone', this particular type of asbestos is now understood to be among the most deadly, and potentially up to a hundred times more hazardous than white asbestos. Speculation over the potential health risks of asbestos was first made at the turn of the twentieth century, but for decades it continued to be widely employed in the insulation of machinery and buildings, and used with cement for pavement, roads and sports grounds. Such was the demand, with Britain one of the largest importers of it from South Africa and Australia, that its discovery in Pilbara fed a Gold Rush-style boom in this outlying part of the outback in 1920s and 1930s.

One group of speculators, headed by Lang Hancock (who subsequently also discovered the world's largest iron ore deposit in the Pilbara region),

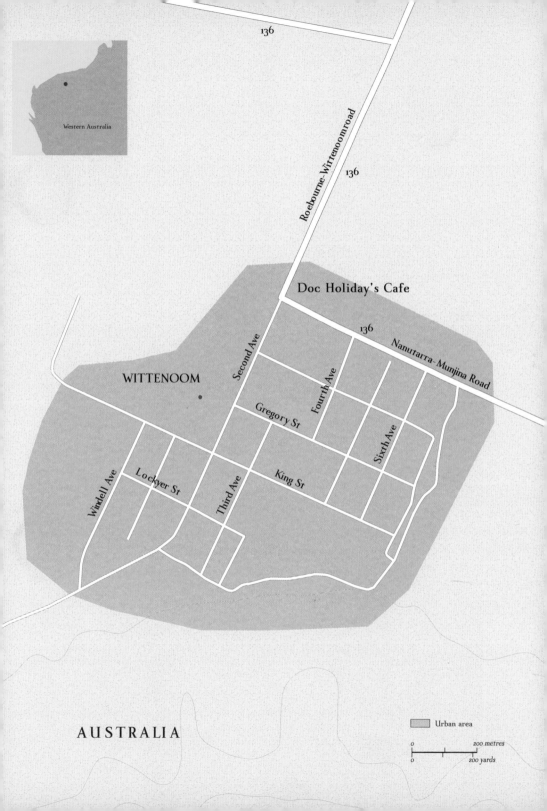

136

Roebourne–Wittenoom road

136

Doc Holiday's Cafe

136

Nanutarra–Munjina Road

Second Ave

WITTENOOM

Fourth Ave

Gregory St

Sixth Ave

Windell Ave

Lockyer St

Third Ave

King St

Western Australia

AUSTRALIA

Urban area

0   200 metres
0   200 yards

established an asbestos mine and crushing plant at Wittenoom Gorge in 1938. Five years later, while initially retaining a stake in the business, Lang sold the mine to one of Australia's larger and most established companies, CSR (Colonial Sugar Refining Company), and what had been a rather tinpot operation expanded. An entire town, Wittenoom, rose up to house miners just a few miles away from the mine.

Below: Much of Wittenoom still stands despite being abandoned and taken off the grid.

Following a damning medical report, the mine was finally closed in 1966 and with it went the town. Half a century on, its buildings are empty

of people but they remain riddled with asbestos. Tailings lie all around and open to the elements. Particles of the mineral are carried from them through the air by scorching summer winds and drift down into the waters of local rivers. In 2007 the Australian goverment officially closed Witternoom. Taking it off power and communication lines, they went so far as to remove it from official maps, thereby rendering this once busy town a 'place' no more to all intents and purpose.

Ani, Kars

Ruins of one-time capital of the Armenian Empire

Kars [Turkey]

40° 30' 39"N
43° 34' 0"E

In the Old Testament, 2 Samuel, 1:25, King David, mourning the loss of Saul and Saul's son Jonathan, cries out in despair, 'How the mighty have fallen.' Seven hundred years ago no one consulting that biblical passage in one of the '1001 churches' of Ani could possibly have imagined just how far this mightiest of Armenian cities would fall. Nor, for that matter, the suffering this landlocked kingdom would endure in the intervening period. Today Ani is surrounded by Turkey to its west, Georgia to the north and Azerbaijan to its east and south, along with Iran, and all that remains of it are some impressive ruins standing on a grassy plateau beside the Akhurian River. In the current geopolitical layout these are situated on the Turkish side of the Armenian–Turkish border. Having come close to being eradicated completely, Ani has finally been treated to some conservation work in the last decade, and at the time of writing has been nominated as a UNESCO World Heritage Site. But it's not that long ago that permission was required to visit Ani, marooned as it then was in a military no man's land, and photography of the ruins forbidden by the Turkish government.

A settlement since prehistoric times, it became the capital of the Bagratid kings of Armenia in AD 961 when Ashot III moved his court from Kars, a city about 28 miles further west, and one that ultimately ended up weathering rather better than its usurper. Under Ashot's successors, Smbat II and, especially, Gagik I, Ani evolved into a prosperous walled metropolis, a regal and mercantile capital to rival Constantinople. And one seemingly noted for its religious piety since it was generally

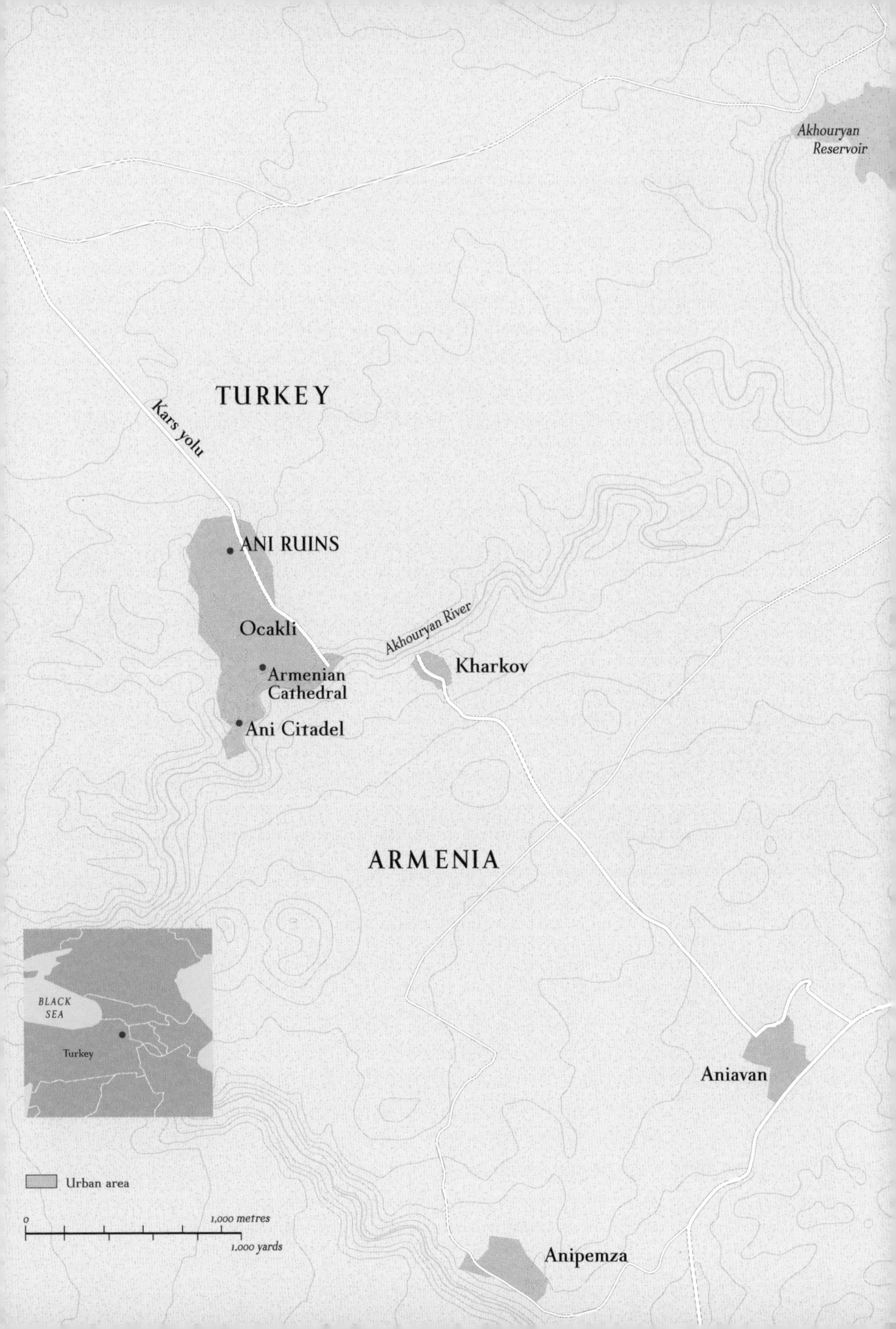

Akhouryan
Reservoir

TURKEY

Kars yolu

● ANI RUINS

Ocakli

Akhouryan River

Kharkov

● Armenian
Cathedral

● Ani Citadel

ARMENIA

BLACK
SEA

Turkey

Aniavan

Urban area

0   1,000 metres
                    1,000 yards

Anipemza

acclaimed as 'the city of 1001 churches', among them a majestic domed cathedral dedicated to the Blessed Virgin by the esteemed Armenian architect Trdat.

Located on the Silk Route between Europe and China, Ani would see its population swell to 100,000. But disputes among the Bagratid dynasty ultimately led to the city being claimed by the Byzantium Empire in 1045. Nineteen years later, it was sacked by the Turks, who converted Trdat's cathedral into a mosque. The city rallied, though, passing through Kurdish and Georgian hands, before, *c.*1237, the Mongols arrived and laid waste to Ani, burning its buildings and slaughtering its citizens. Ani would rise again, only to be hit by an earthquake in 1319 from which it never fully recovered. By the middle of the eighteenth century it was all but uninhabited, and was abandoned entirely not long after that. It suffered its final indignity in 1957 when half of the Church of the Holy Redeemer, said to have been built in 1035 by Prince Ablgharib Pahlavid to house a fragment of the True Cross, collapsed after it was struck by lightning. It, like much else in Ani, remains in an extremely fragile state. But what clings on – tumbled-down sections of walls, archways, turrets, towers and domes and crumbing citadels, churches and mosques – adds up to palimpsest of more than a thousand years of Armenian civilization.

Left: The crumbling remains of the Church of the Holy Redeemer, fragile testament to the once thriving capital.

CONCRETE CITY

GARDEN CITY OF THE ANTHRACITE REGION

PENNSYLVANIA [UNITED STATES]

41° 11' 21"N
75° 58' 34"W

North-eastern Pennsylvania is home to the largest known deposits of anthracite coal in America. In the opening decades of the nineteenth century, and in the aftermath of the industrial revolution, demand for coal saw the region boom as speculators rushed to exploit this precious natural resource. Fortunes were made here from mining and the railroads, but the spoils were far from equally shared. While coal companies and railroad shareholders grew rich and built themselves elegant mansions in leafy districts far removed from their mines, their labour force of mostly new immigrants from Germany, Wales, Ireland, Italy and Eastern Europe toiled in appalling conditions and lived in overcrowded 'patch towns'. These were company-owned settlements of cheaply and shoddily built wood-frame and board houses, with a store, a church and perhaps a tavern, all controlled by the company, and usually on land close to the mine or breaking plant.

Elsewhere in America and Europe, however, industrialists were beginning to realize that better living and working conditions might make for better and more productive workers, yielding, in turn, greater profits for the company in the long term. Spurred on in part by industrial unrest and the examples of other enlightened industrial settlements, Pennsylvania's coal companies started to invest in new employee housing schemes of their own in the run-up to the First World War.

By far and away the most ambitious new design was Concrete City, at Nanticoke, Pennsylvania. This was developed in 1911 by the Delaware, Lackawanna and Western (DL&W), a rail and mining concern with a network of tracks and coal interests that stretched from Scranton to

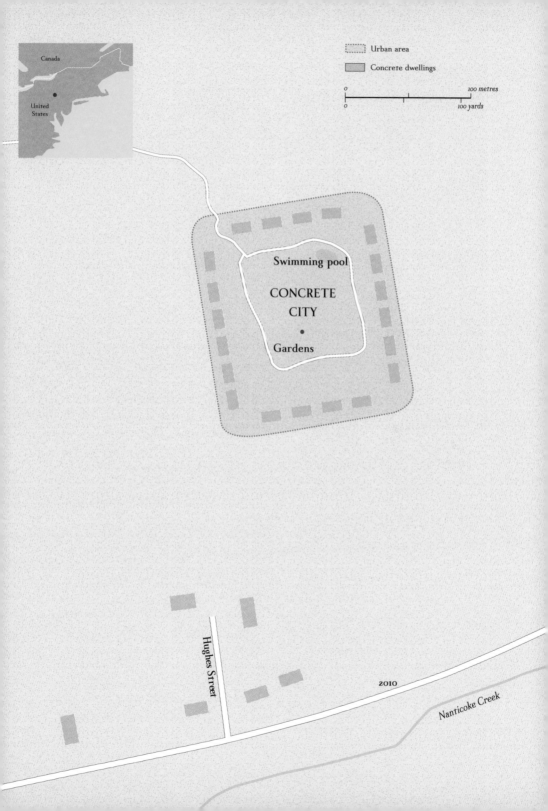

Canada

United
States

Urban area

Concrete dwellings

0   100 metres

0   100 yards

Swimming pool

CONCRETE
CITY

Gardens

Hughes Street

2010

Nanticoke Creek

Hoboken and the Hudson River – and one of the largest employers in the Nanticoke area. Lying on a thirty-nine-acre tract of land within sight of the DL&W's Truesdale Colliery, it was hailed as 'the Garden City of the Anthracite Region'. William Morris, the English artist, textile designer and political campaigner, is credited with coining the term 'garden city', but the concept is most closely associated with Ebenezer Howard, who used it to espouse a new type of purpose-built town that combined the best of the urban and the rural in his influential 1898 book *To-Morrow: A Peaceful Path to Real Reform*.

The new town was certainly technologically advanced. The inner shells of its twenty double-block detached houses were inventively fabricated from poured concrete, with steps, partitions, floors and roofs in reinforced concrete. With seven generously sized rooms, each house came with running water and a hot-water tank, and a laundry-cum-bathtub that also served as the kitchen sink. Smartly trimmed with green paint, they were neatly arranged to face a central courtyard, and four-foot-wide sidewalks dotted with lampposts separated the houses from the street. Trees and shrubs were plentiful and window boxes were fitted to the front window of every house. DL&W would go on to present awards for the best-kept gardens in the development. By the summer of 1914, the company had added a concrete swimming pool, a playground and a baseball diamond for the residents to its score of facilities.

The town was not without problems. There were persistent issues with damp and with peeling paint, as the houses proved difficult to heat. Shirts hanging in the closets, former tenants reported, were sometimes found frozen stiff in the morning in the winter months. What finally did for Concrete City, however, was sanitation. It was equipped with basic concrete outhouses at its inception, and in 1924 its owners, now the Glen Alden Coal Company, were required by the township to install a whole new sewer system. Baulking at an estimated cost of $200,000 to undertake these improvements, the company opted to cut its losses, its board voting to dispense with the settlement. Explosives experts were hired and the task of demolishing the town began in earnest in December 1924. But some weeks in, and having seen the use of a hundred sticks of dynamite, most of Concrete City amazingly still stood rock-solid. With the demolition men having managed to inflict only the most superficial damage to its buildings, the company decided to abandon it rather than spend any more money attempting to destroy them.

It has since been utilized for many years as a training ground by local emergency service rescue teams, and its houses' once pristine, whitewashed walls are crumbling, riddled with bullet holes and plastered with graffiti, while its former prize-winning gardens are a mess of tangled weeds and fly-tipped trash. But a historical marker – placed here by the Pennsylvania Historical and Museum Commission, the same organization that saved what remains from wrecking balls back in 1992 – alerts those who might otherwise take it for a festering eyesore to the architectural significance of this pioneering American housing scheme.

VAROSHA

ABANDONED TOURIST RESORT

FAMAGUSTA [CYPRUS]

35° 6' 21" N
33° 57' 19" E

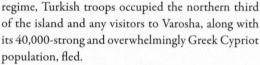

Varosha in Famagusta was described by some as 'the French Riviera of Cyprus', its sandy beaches and high-end, high-rise hotels frequented by the glamorous, wealthy and famous in the 1960s. Brigitte Bardot, Richard Burton and Elizabeth Taylor, who counted the Argo Hotel on J.F.K. Avenue as a particular favourite, were among those who sealed its reputation as a destination for the international jet set. But in the summer of 1974, after decades of ethnic tension and agitation from the Greek military

Above: In the early 1970s, it was the most important tourist resort in Cyprus, famous for its sandy beaches. Now empty and uninhabited, Varosha is fenced off and held in captivity.

regime, Turkish troops occupied the northern third of the island and any visitors to Varosha, along with its 40,000-strong and overwhelmingly Greek Cypriot population, fled.

For forty-plus years Turkish soldiers were just about the only people to step upon its sands, and the dunes were gradually appropriated, in the absence of crowds of sunbathers, by bales of nesting sea turtles. Mother Nature was similarly to have her way with Varosha's buildings and streets, the prickly pear and other untamable vegetation claiming pavements and clambering up the walls of war-damaged and deserted homes and concrete holiday apartment blocks. In other respects time could almost be said to have stood still here.

Though this area remained out of bounds, some of those who have ventured inside this ghost resort found closets full of once fashionable 1970s clothes and a car showroom full of rusting models of vehicles not seen on the forecourts since the end of OPEC's oil embargo.

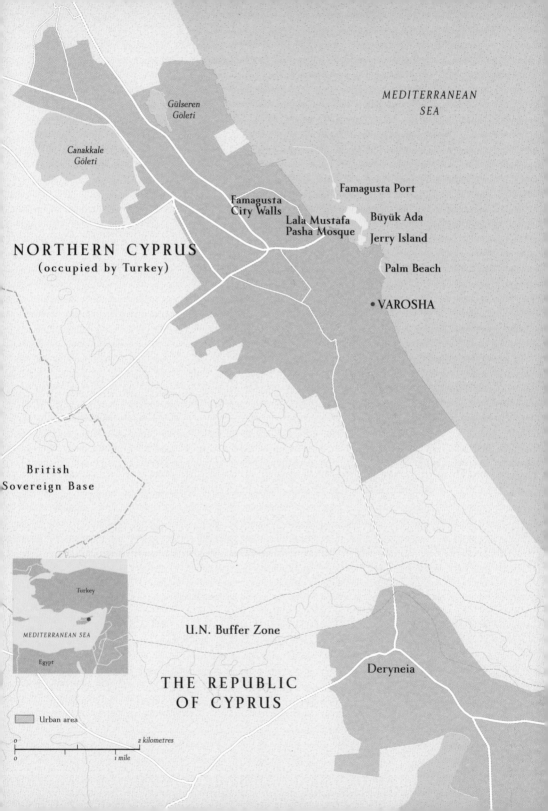

MEDITERRANEAN
SEA

*Gülseren
Göleti*

*Canakkale
Göleti*

Famagusta Port

Famagusta
City Walls

Lala Mustafa
Pasha Mosque

Büyük Ada

Jerry Island

NORTHERN CYPRUS
(occupied by Turkey)

Palm Beach

•VAROSHA

British
Sovereign Base

Turkey

MEDITERRANEAN SEA

Egypt

U.N. Buffer Zone

Deryneia

THE REPUBLIC
OF CYPRUS

Urban area

0   2 kilometres

0   1 mile

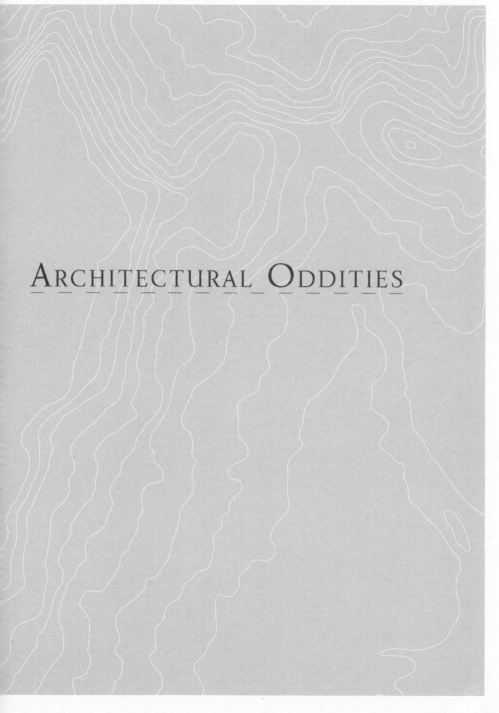

ARCHITECTURAL ODDITIES

Maryhill Stonehenge

Concrete Stonehenge

Washington State [United States]

45° 41' 39"N
120° 48' 21"W

To this day we still do not know who, why or to what ends Stonehenge was really built. The ancient stone circle on the chalk downlands of Salisbury Plain in Wiltshire remains something of an archaeological enigma. Over the centuries, antiquaries, field historians, scientists and folklorists have outlined theories as to its origins and former uses. Stonehenge has erroneously been claimed as a Roman ruin, held up as the Platonic ideal of architecture and besmirched as a site of bloody slaughter. Current thinking variously fingers the landmark as a burial ground, a lunar temple, an astronomical clock, a place of healing and, most improbably of all, as a landing pad for UFOs. To our Victorian and Edwardian forebears, Stonehenge was most readily associated with the druids, who were widely held to be its architects. This idea was put about by the eighteenth-century antiquary William Stukeley, but is entirely discounted by archaeologists today, though contemporary disciples of this pre-Christian pagan faith still regard it as sacred and continue to observe the winter and summer solstices there, as they have done for the last two hundred or so years.

If the roots of the original are lost in the mists of time, the whys and wherefores of a full-size replica in concrete at Maryhill in Washington State, USA, are, by comparison, pretty straightforward, if naturally a tad unusual. The Maryhill Stonehenge was the brainchild of the road maker Samuel Hill – a figure posthumously profiled in a Seattle newspaper under the headline, 'Northwest Visionary or Paranoid Eccentric?'. A biography of Hill was, meanwhile, subtitled 'The Prince of Castle Nowhere'.

The son of a Quaker doctor and born in Deep River, North Carolina, in

WASHINGTON

97

STONEHENGE
MEMORIAL

14

Highway 30

Columbia River

Miller
Island

Biggs Junction

OREGON

Canada

United
States

Urban area

0   2 kilometres

0   1 mile

1857, Hill cut his teeth as a teenage railways surveyor before studying law at Harvard University and becoming a legal adviser to the Great Northern Railway of Saint Paul, Minnesota. By the turn of the twentieth century, though, and having grown personally wealthy through stock speculation, Hill surmised that gas and roads, rather than rail and steam, were the future. He headed west to Seattle, where he served as the president of the Seattle Gas and Electricity Company, the Washington State Good Roads Association and, later, the Pacific Highway Association. Not everything about Hill was on the straight and narrow, however. He had numerous extra-marital affairs before separating from his wife and in his twilight years was convinced that all manner of 'anarchists', 'communists' and common 'burglars' were out to get him.

Nevertheless, Quakerism was Hill's creed and, though reluctantly supporting America's involvement in the First World War, he was a lifelong pacifist. In 1907, Hill acquired 6,000 acres of land in Klickitat, Washington State, with the aim of establishing a Quaker agricultural community he eventually called Maryhill, after his daughter Mary. To attract working people to his 'promised land' overlooking the Columbia River, he would fund an inn and a museum and art gallery in the following year and began laying a series of model roads, largely to impress upon the legislators in Oregon the benefits of asphalt and paving.

Ultimately the Maryhill settlement was a failure as far as farmsteads were concerned. A fire destroyed what few houses had been built before anyone was tempted to move to this remote outpost. But in 1918 the road man initiated a plan to erect a memorial here to those who'd lost their lives in the then recently ended conflict. Believing that Stonehenge had served as a place of human sacrifice, he decided a full-scale model would make an appropriate monument to the fallen of Klickitat County.

Hill initially aimed for his henge to be built in local sand and rubble stone, but when this proved too unwieldy, he turned to reinforced concrete – a material then rapidly coming into its own in the construction of new highways and high-rise buildings. He also took a leaf out of Henry Ford's mass-production methods, and the megaliths were assembled from pre-pressed uniform blocks of concrete. Each was finessed with a special lumpy coating to lend the structure the weathered look of its English antecedent. The construction of the original Stonehenge was long and complex. Modern carbon dating confirms that a simple earthwork ditch was established in around 2900 BC, and best estimates put the journey from that to the full ring of rocks at around five hundred back-breaking years of continuous labour. Inevitably Hill's version, a product of early

Above: The concrete standing stones of Samuel Hill.

twentieth-century American ingenuity, took considerably less time and effort to knock up. Nevertheless, it was 1929 before it was finished. Hill, increasingly plagued by paranoia, was to die just two years later. His ashes were interned in a crypt a short distance from the memorial, this last resting place marked, since 1955, by a more modest granite monument to Hill himself.

If both crypt and henge keep somewhat lonely vigils on grassy hilltop bluffs with only sagebrush and some wind turbines for company, the Maryhill Stonehenge certainly attracts pilgrims. But as it's aligned to the astronomical horizon rather than the solstice sunrises like Stonehenge itself, and the surrounding hills obscure the horizon somewhat, it makes for a rather poor spot for pagan worship. As a war memorial, however, it's odd, and oddly affecting, the spareness of its eyrie locality and fine view over the river far below only serving to heighten thoughts of mortality and loss.

Spijkenisse

The 'real' fictional euro bridges
Rotterdam [Netherlands]

51° 51' 3" N
4° 20' 11" E

Bridges are liminal structures. They lie between two banks and between land and water. Their metaphorical potential has never been lost on artists, poets, novelists and harmonic vocal folk duos with choppy liquids on their minds. For politicians, too (or at least their speechwriters), a bridge is a gift that rarely stops giving, symbolically speaking.

And so it was that in 1996, when the European Monetary Institute (EMI) was casting around for designs for the continent's new common currency, the euro, it was seduced by an offering from Robert Kalina which leant heavily on bridges through the ages. Along with doors and gateways, as it happened. Kalina's choice of imagery was praised by the EMI for conveying a sense of architectural progress while also alluding to the linking up of different nations. Its other visual details, meanwhile, hammered home the whole idea of doors to international trade and travel opening with the adoption of a single currency.

However, there was just one small problem with Kalina's bridges. Some of them looked suspiciously like spans famous across Europe, if not around the globe. Charming as it might have been to recall a day strolling along the Seine or drifting over the Arno, while you actually shopped for groceries in Brussels or Bratislava, the EMI was concerned that nations lacking a bridge of note to include on any note would feel hard done by. In any case, initially, there were also to be twelve participating countries and yet only seven notes. With only one bridge inked in for each note, someone was destined to get left out. The EMI therefore asked Kalina to modify his designs to embody general styles of bridges – the Roman, the Gothic,

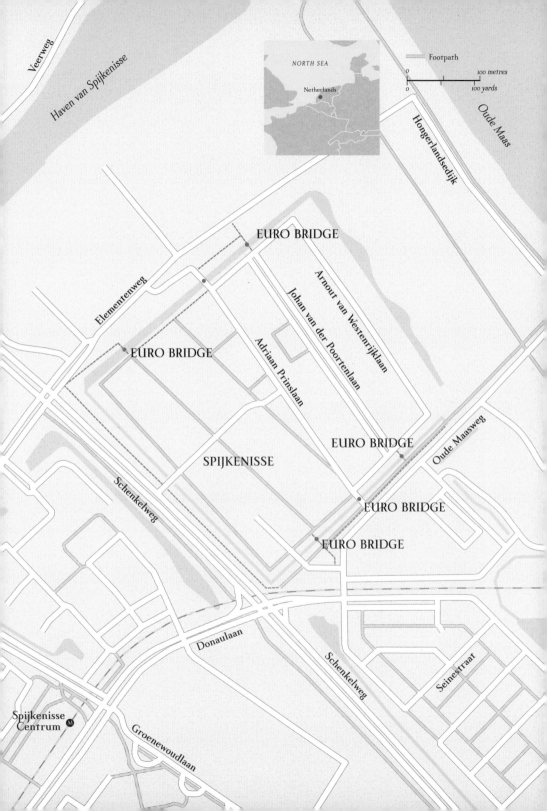

NORTH SEA

Netherlands

Footpath

0   100 metres
0   100 yards

Veerweg

Haven van Spijkenisse

Hongerlandsedijk

Oude Maas

EURO BRIDGE

Elementenweg

EURO BRIDGE

Arnout van Westenrijklaan

Johan van der Poortenlaan

Adriaan Prinslaan

EURO BRIDGE

Oude Maasweg

SPIJKENISSE

EURO BRIDGE

Schenkelweg

EURO BRIDGE

Donaulaan

Schenkelweg

Seinestraat

Spijkenisse
Centrum Ⓜ

Groenewoudlaan

the contemporary and so on – but not to represent any extant examples. He readily complied and euro notes of varying denominations went into circulation in 2002 carrying the images of seven different, brightly coloured and specifically fictional bridges on the backs of them.

Nine years on, however, the Dutch artist Robin Stam, having mused on the notion of creating a work based on something that people used unthinkingly every day, embarked on a project to bring the euro note bridges to life. Worried he might be arrested for counterfeiting, Stam first sought the blessing of the European Central Bank, which informed him that building copies of bridges on the banknotes would be fine; copying the notes themselves, less so. With that settled, he secured the backing of a developer of a new housing estate and over the next couple of years set about

erecting each of the seven bridges in a suburb of Spijkenisse in southern Holland. Staying true to the vivid hues of Kalina's print designs, Stam's bridges appear positively surreal and rather kitsch, if anything, amidst the estate. Rendered in 3-D and mostly in gaudily coloured concrete, they look more like exhibits from the Euro Disney theme park than the archetypes of centuries of civil engineering which Kalina perhaps first intended. But just as some of the 'real' bridges that inspired those banknote counterparts have become visitor attractions, so, too, have Stam's real versions of the fakes. The consequence is that Spijkenisse, previously overlooked in favour of the livelier offerings of near metropolitan neighbour Rotterdam, has today earned its own place on the Dutch tourist map.

Below: From illustration to engineering, one of the Euro-note crossings at Spijkenisse.

KABAYAN

THE IBALOI MUMMY CAVES

BENGUET [PHILIPPINES]

16° 37' 1"N
120° 49' 36"E

In ancient times, when life could be nasty, brutish and short and doctors' cures could be almost as deadly as any disease, death was a constant presence. Unable to do much for the terminally ill other than speed their eventual demise, and sometimes doing so exceedingly brutally, our ancestors nevertheless set a lot of store on preparing for the afterlife. The death rituals of the Ibaloi tribe of Benguet Province in the Philippines were certainly involved and all the more strikingly since they required the considerable and active participation of the dying, too. For the Ibaloi, like the ancient Egyptians, mummified their dead, but they used a rather unique embalming technique.

Above: All wrapped up, the Kabayan mummies in situ.

Their favoured method of preservation was essentially to cure the corpses with smoke and dry out the bodies until all that was left was a kind of desiccated husk of a human being. However, the process of dehydration began well before death. The terminally ill, accepting their fate with a certain equanimity, would drink beverages heavily laced with salt, a fatal poison if ingested in anything other than modest quantities. Once the person was dead, the body was washed down with herbs and tobacco smoke was blown over it and into the mouth of the deceased by mourners before being hung above a smouldering fire for weeks on end. When mummification was complete the dead were ceremoniously laid to rest in oval-shaped wooden coffins carved with decorations, and buried deep inside cave tombs.

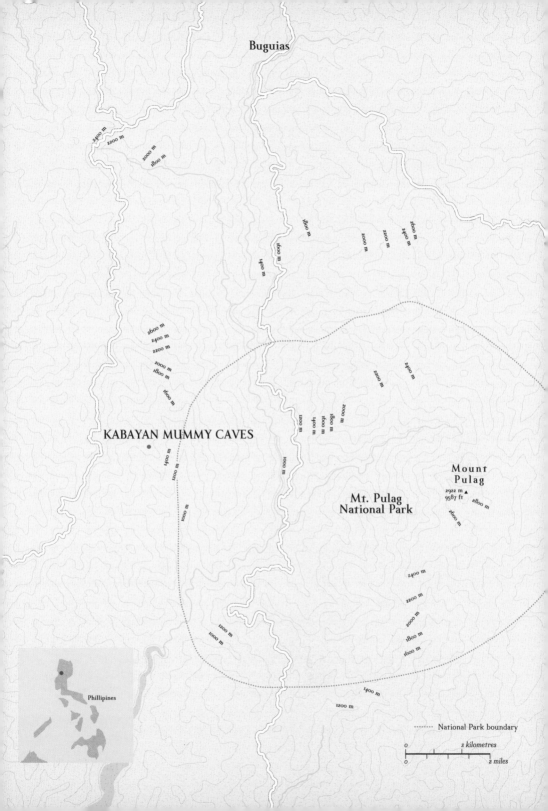

Buguias

2400 m
2200 m
2000 m
1800 m

1800 m

1600 m
1400 m

2600 m
2000 m
2200 m
2400 m

2600 m
2400 m
2200 m
2000 m
1800 m
1600 m

2400 m
2200 m

2000 m
1800 m
1600 m
1400 m
1200 m

KABAYAN MUMMY CAVES

1400 m
1200 m

1200 m
1000 m

1000 m

Mount
Pulag

2922 m
9587 ft ▲ 2800 m

Mt. Pulag
National Park

2600 m

2400 m

2200 m

2000 m

1800 m

1600 m

1200 m
1000 m

1400 m

1200 m

Phillipines

National Park boundary

0   2 kilometres

0   2 miles

Santurio Madonna Della Corona

Chapel hangs midway down a sheer cliffside
Verona [Italy]

45° 38' 57" N
10° 51' 23" E

If God, at least according to the Old Testament, took a dim view of the sky-seeking Tower of Babel, the urge to reach heavenwards has remained a persistent feature of Christian architecture, perhaps reaching its apogee in the vaulting steeples and spires of Gothic cathedrals and churches of medieval times. The Santuario Madonna della Corona, or Sanctuary of the Lady of the Crown, couldn't get much higher. This church in Spiazzi, in the province of Verona, is built into the bare rock face of Mount Baldo in the Italian Alps and lodged, vulnerably, on a shelf of stone some 2,539 feet above sea level. Far below it is the valley of the Adige River and above it only cliffs and sky; heaven, by almost anyone's definition.

Pious hermits associated with the Abbey of St Zeno in Verona and seemingly undaunted by heights and treacherous mountain paths are believed to have established a religious retreat on Baldo in around AD 1000. A monastery was certainly in existence in the vicinity by the thirteenth century. The origins of the church, though, are, by holy tradition, typically dated to 1522. It was then apparently that a statue of the Lady of Corona from Rhodes is said to have been 'miraculously transported' here through 'angelic intervention' at the precise moment that this Greek island was overcome by the Islamic forces of Suleiman I. Eight years on a chapel was built as a shrine to this divine intervention and a century later a grander structure was erected, various incarnations of which have existed ever since.

The last major work on the church occurred in the 1970s. Having undergone a neo-Gothic makeover and much else besides in the Victorian age, the church was pronounced structurally unsound and almost

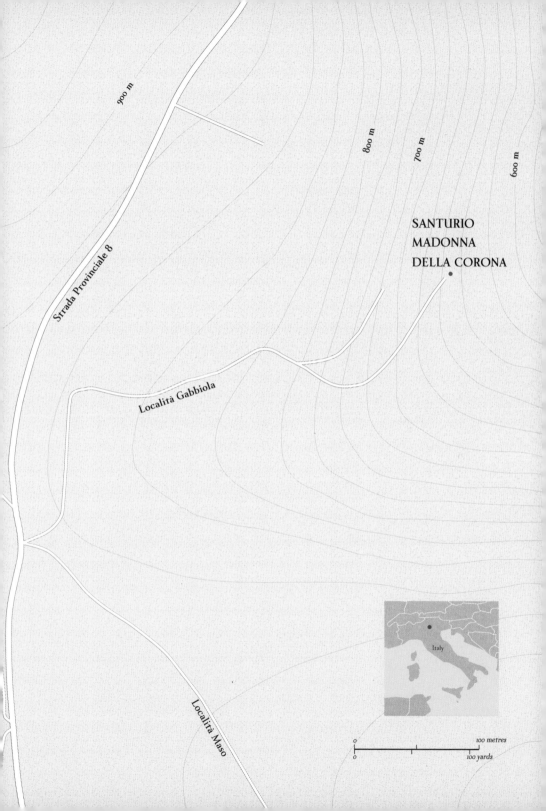

900 m

800 m

700 m

600 m

Strada Provinciale 8

SANTURIO
MADONNA
DELLA CORONA

Località Gabbiola

Località Maso

Italy

0   100 metres

0   100 yards

ATLAS OF IMPROBABLE PLACES

completely demolished before being painstakingly, and sympathetically, reconfigured by the architect Guido Tisato between 1975 and 1978. The pathways, equally, are far less precarious than in ages past but a pilgrimage from Brentino Belluno requires the devout to undertake a suitable testing ascent up some 1,540 steps.

As its own website boasts, this footpath offers a chance 'to understand and experience the value and meaning of suffering' as it takes about an hour and half to reach the church shrine itself. The round trip is, in turn, described as 'a pleasant feeling for the body and the spirit'.

Left: Santurio Madonna della Corona clings to the cliff face.

London Bridge, Lake Havasu

The 1831 London Bridge
Arizona [United States]

34° 28' 17" N
114° 20' 51" E

Lake Havasu City lies by the Colorado River on a 45-mile stretch of clear water amid the desert peaks of western Arizona. The landscape is characterized by arid expanses of sand, bare red rock and eroded sediment, while the local flora – cat's claw, bursage and mesquite – pokes out of the dusty ground like bristles on a hog. A more unlikely setting for a nineteenth-century British architectural landmark can't really be imagined. And yet John Rennie's London Bridge has called Lake Havasu City home since 1971.

The bridge's fantastical journey from murky Southwark in south London to dust-dry Mojave County began in 1967, when the Corporation of London put it up for sale. Fashioned for posterity in 130,000 tons of granite in 1831, the span was calculated to be sinking at a rate of an eighth of an inch a year by the early 1960s. Its eventual purchasers (and also the founding fathers of Lake Havasu City) were Robert P. McCulloch and C.V. Wood. McCulloch was a flamboyant millionaire oil baron and chainsaw manufacturing magnate who in 1963 hatched a scheme to build a new city out in the desert. The bridge, shipped in pieces across the Atlantic and reassembled, became the centrepiece of a visitor attraction called the English village, a mini 'ye olde London town', which in its heyday in the 1970s and 1980s could boast a traditional British pub that served beer in tankards and a red double-decker bus converted into an ice-cream parlour.

Overleaf: The 1831 London Bridge that formerly spanned the River Thames in London, England until it was dismantled in 1967. Relocated to Arizona, it is now a central attraction in Lake Havasu City.

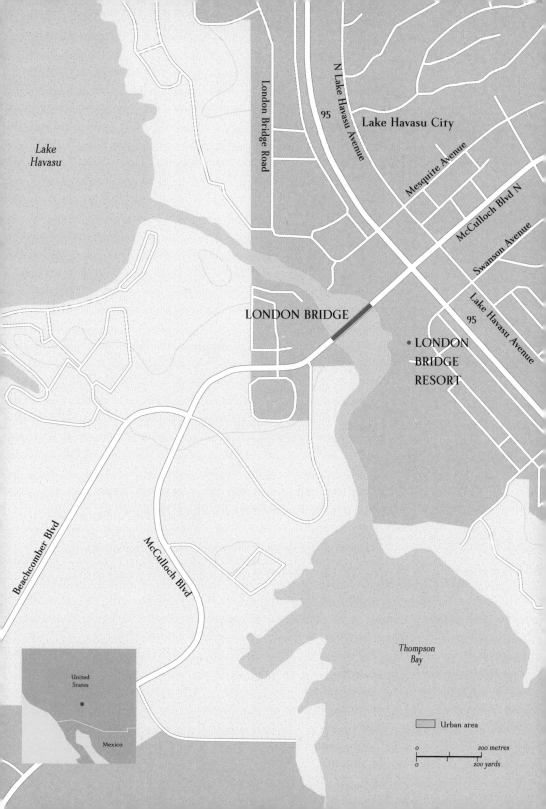

Lake
Havasu

London Bridge Road

N Lake Havasu Avenue

95

Lake Havasu City

Mesquite Avenue

McCulloch Blvd N

Swanson Avenue

LONDON BRIDGE

Lake Havasu Avenue

95

• LONDON
BRIDGE
RESORT

Beachcomber Blvd

McCulloch Blvd

Thompson
Bay

United
States

Mexico

☐ Urban area

0   200 metres

0   200 yards

THE AFRICAN RENAISSANCE MONUMENT

CONTROVERSIAL SYMBOL OF INDEPENDENCE

SENEGAL [WEST AFRICA]

14° 45' 52" N
17° 21' 57" W

The French writer Guy de Maupassant famously hated the Eiffel Tower. He disliked it so much that he regularly took lunch in the Tower's second-floor restaurant, claiming that it was the only place in Paris where he couldn't see 'this tall skinny pyramid of iron ladders, this giant and disgraceful skeleton'. The African Renaissance Monument, deliberately conceived to provide Dakar in Senegal with a landmark as imposing, is equally difficult to avoid. The statue is 160 feet high as it is, but on its natural pedestal, the top of an extinct volcano, it's taller than the Statue of Liberty and Christ the Redeemer in Rio de Janeiro, towering some 490 feet above this most westerly of African port cities. If lacking a restaurant, it does have a lift, which for a fee allows ascents to the head of one of its three figures, where spectacular views of Dakar can be enjoyed and where the statue itself is, shall we say, less foregrounded.

The monument was the brainchild of Senegal's octogenarian former president Abdoulaye Wade. Based on a sketch that first appeared in *A Destiny for Africa*, a book Wade published early in his lengthy, and more latterly controversial, political career, the bronze statue is a representation of a triumphant African family. At the centre is a giant barrel-chested man, rippling with muscles. At the man's rear and clinging to one of his tree-trunk-sized arms is a woman with what might politely be described as ample breasts and strangely windswept braided hair, in a noticeably less than ample dress. In the curve of the man's other arm, and practically sitting on a bicep as bulbous as a dromedary's hump, is a small child who points out to the Atlantic Ocean ahead, his left arm outstretched and tiny index

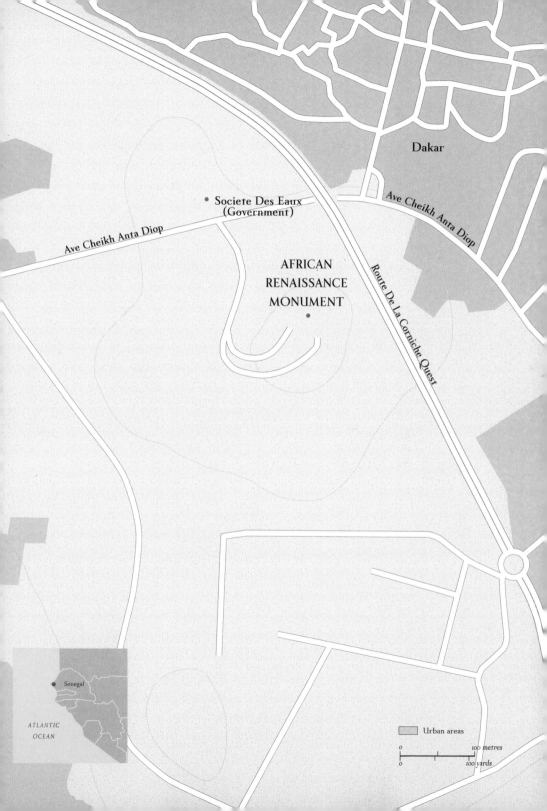

Dakar

Societe Des Eaux
(Government)

Ave Cheikh Anta Diop

Ave Cheikh Anta Diop

AFRICAN
RENAISSANCE
MONUMENT

Route De La Corniche Ouest

Senegal

ATLANTIC
OCEAN

Urban areas

0   100 metres
0   100 yards

finger teasing the briny air. Unveiled on 4 April 2010 to coincide with the fiftieth anniversary of Senegal's independence from France, the monument was described by Wade as embodying 'Africa emerging from darkness, from five centuries of slavery and two centuries of colonialism'.

Critics in Senegal, however, lined up to denounce it as 'the product of a power-drunk president' and 'a colossal financial, political and aesthetic scandal'. The near-nudity of the female figure in a predominantly Muslim nation caused enormous offence in particular, with one imam even issuing a fatwa against it for idolatry. Statues of this scale rarely come cheap and the African Renaissance Monument would cost some $27 million at a time when, according to the World Bank, 47 per cent of the Senegalese population were living below the poverty line. That disjunction is graphically illustrated in the area immediately below the statue itself: Wade's one-child clan stand, shimmering and god-like, above squatter camps and piles of dumped waste and festering rubbish. Its expense may possibly have seemed more palatable had Wade himself not announced that, having conceived the thing, he intended to retain a 35 per cent stake in any revenues generated from elevator tolls and entrance fees.

The job of converting Wade's basic conceit into a statue had fallen to the Senegalese architect Pierre Goudiaby Atepa and the Romanian-born sculptor Virgil Magherusan. It is Magherusan who is credited with the sculpture's grandiose, socialist realist form – a style propagated by the Soviet Union under Stalin and categorized by its rigorous optimism and fetish of physical labour.

To the further dismay of Wade's detractors, the monument's construction was handled by a team of fifty North Koreans from Mansudae Overseas Projects, a Pyongyang company. Founded in 1959, six years after the end of the Korean War, Mansudae is perhaps the world's biggest art factory. It employs about 4,000 people, of whom around 1,000 are artists specially selected from the country's finest academies, its main role being to churn out propaganda paintings, posters, murals and statues for the North Korean government. Its artists alone have a state-sanctioned monopoly on portraying – and deifying – the ruling Kim family dynasty. Here, though, as Wade's government were unable to meet the final price of its construction, the North Koreans accepted payment in kind in land, which they later sold for a profit.

Right: Statuary on a scale seldom seen outside North Korea. Its size was just one of the controversies surrounding its inception.

The Fields of the Wood

North Carolina [United States]

35° 7' 13" N
84° 15' 0" W

Regardless of our faith or creed or lack of faith entirely, the Ten Commandments remain worthy of consultation from time to time. And where better to gaze upon them than on a real live mountain on a tablet a staggering 300 feet wide and in white concrete characters that are five feet high and four feet wide?

Burger Mountain is the centrepiece of the Fields of the Wood, a 200-acre outdoor biblical theme park in the foothills of the Great Smoky Mountains in Murphy, North Carolina. Its heavenward leaning, grassy slope is adorned with what is officially the World's Largest Ten Commandments. Its summit, reached by 358 steps, is crowned by an observation platform called the New Testament Outlook, where fresh mountain air can be inhaled and North Carolina, eastern Tennessee and northern Georgia spied on clearer days. Elsewhere in the park there is a plethora of other religious monuments and markers. There is a full-size baptismal pool. A scale replica of the Garden Tomb of Joseph of Arimathea, where the Gospels state Jesus's body was buried after the crucifixion, replete with a large 'rolled away' stone sitting outside its entrance. And picking up the mountain motif there is also an ersatz Golgotha, topped with a trio of wooden crosses. Its visitor centre shop sells godly gifts, ten-inch-long plastic rulers with 'He's the Ruler' printed on them among them. The Ten Commandments, though, easily and almost inevitably trumps almost any of these other attractions. The whole thing is the legacy of the Pentecostal evangelist Ambrose Jessup (A.J.) Tomlinson, a former Quaker employed as a colporteur for the Bible Society of America.

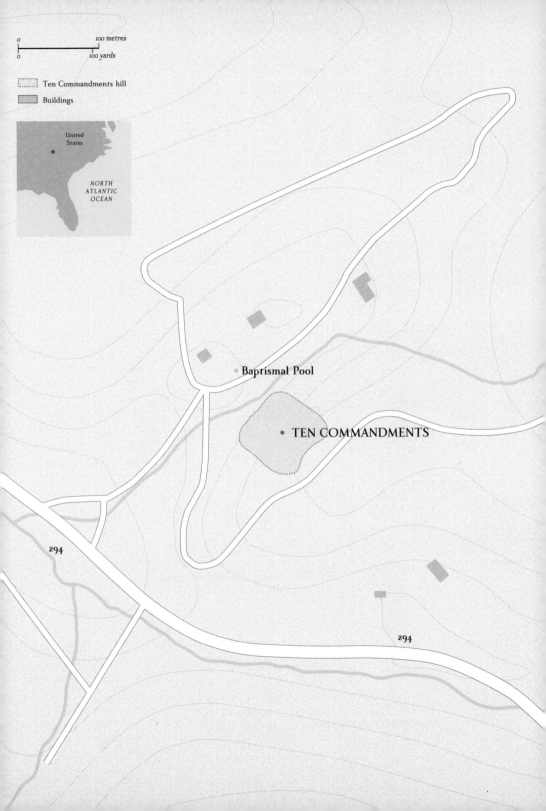

100 metres
100 yards

Ten Commandments hill
Buildings

United
States

NORTH
ATLANTIC
OCEAN

Baptismal Pool

• TEN COMMANDMENTS

294

294

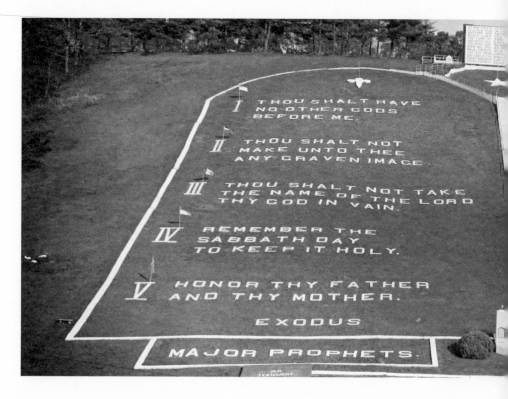

THOU SHALT HAVE
NO OTHER GODS
BEFORE ME.

THOU SHALT NOT
MAKE UNTO THEE
ANY GRAVEN IMAGE.

THOU SHALT NOT TAKE
THE NAME OF THE LORD
THY GOD IN VAIN.

REMEMBER THE
SABBATH DAY
TO KEEP IT HOLY.

HONOR THY FATHER
AND THY MOTHER.

EXODUS

MAJOR PROPHETS.

Above: The word of God writ large.

Tomlinson spent a couple of years visiting this mountainous region as part of his 'home mission' to distribute bibles, but in 1902 he came into contact with a small Pentecostal community that had established the Holiness Church at Camp Creek in a remote south-western corner of North Carolina. Taken with their message and form of worship, he found himself returning to the Holiness Church meetings again and again and was invited to attend a scripture study session at the cabin home of W. F. Bryant, one of its ministers, scheduled for 13 June 1913, a Saturday. Tomlinson travelled down the previous evening and stayed with the Bryants. The next morning he awoke early, dressed and climbed to the top of the mountain behind their house, where he knelt down to pray. It was then and there that he was 'moved by the Spirit to action', as official sources put it. On returning to the scripture session he threw his lot in with the church, acting first as a pastor and from 1906 as the General Moderator for the Church of God, as it was now renamed. Later, after a split in 1920s that appears to have had as much to do with lax accounting systems as the teachings of the Lord, Tomlinson and his followers continued as the Church of God of Prophesy.

Serving as its 'General Overseer' until his death in 1943, Tomlinson was to plot the erection of the religious 'markers' and monuments at Burger Mountain in the last three years of his life, though their construction was only to begin in earnest in the wake of his passing. The first, the Arise, Shine marker, was laid temporally on 15 November 1940 and on the site of the Bryants' former home and Tomlinson's conversion. Most of the markers and monuments, including the Ten Commandments and a mountain-top altar, were designed by L.S. Rhodes, who strove for the awesome, in the reverential sense of the word. Advertised as 'the Biblical Wonder of the Twentieth Century' in an era when Charlton Heston was breaking box-office records starring as Moses in Cecil B. DeMille's final and most extravagant blockbuster *The Ten Commandments*, the Fields of the Wood Park received copious coverage in such glossy periodicals as *Life* magazine and appeared in numerous cinema newsreels. And not unlike Cecil B. DeMille's film with its cast of thousands and grand sets, costumes and location shoots, it feels at this juncture in the twenty-first century almost a miracle it was ever built at all.

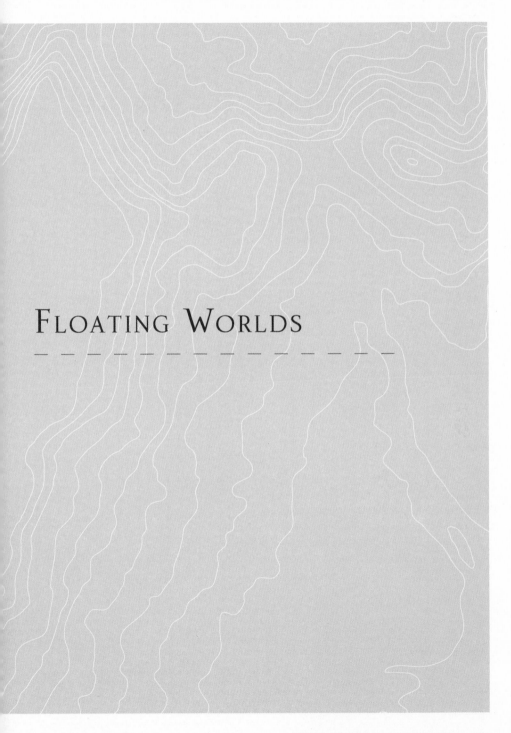

FLOATING WORLDS

The Palm

An artificial island paradise

Dubai [United Arab Emirates]

25° 0' 21" N
54° 59' 21" E

Think of a desert island and as often as not a palm tree will spring to mind. Some lone piece of foliage, say, offering shade to a shipwrecked Robinson Crusoe in rags, or for holidaymakers in a suitably exotic locale to sit under as they sip fruit-heavy chilled drinks and gaze out over golden sands and a blue sea. Paradise incarnate. Earthly bliss. Just imagine then, what a wonder a desert island shaped exactly like a palm tree would be like. Paradise squared? Earthly bliss twice as nice? Well, such an ingenious confection does exist just off the coast of Dubai. The idea, or so the story goes, first came to the ruling Sheikh Mohammed bin Rashid Al Maktoum after he drew a sketch of a leaf and realized that finger-like fronds would provide more beach fronts than simple rounded islands. Constructed entirely from 94 million cubic feet of reclaimed sand, Palm Jumeirah, the first of three luxury manmade island resorts initially proposed, is four times the size of London's Hyde Park. Marketed as the 'Eighth Wonder of the World', the Palm adds some 40 miles to Dubai's coastline, can be seen from space and is made up of seventeen 'fronds' each over a mile in length, fanning out from a central trunk that houses an eight-lane motorway. The palm tree is then topped off with an encircling crescent that also acts as a giant breakwater.

The football star turned global icon David Beckham is widely cited as an early owner of property on Palm Jumeirah, amongst other high-profile celebrities. The financial crash of 2008 and other difficulties, nevertheless, plagued the construction of two further neighbouring islands, Palm Sheikh Ali and Palm Deira.

Overleaf: The fronds of the Palm Tree slowly dissolving into the sea.

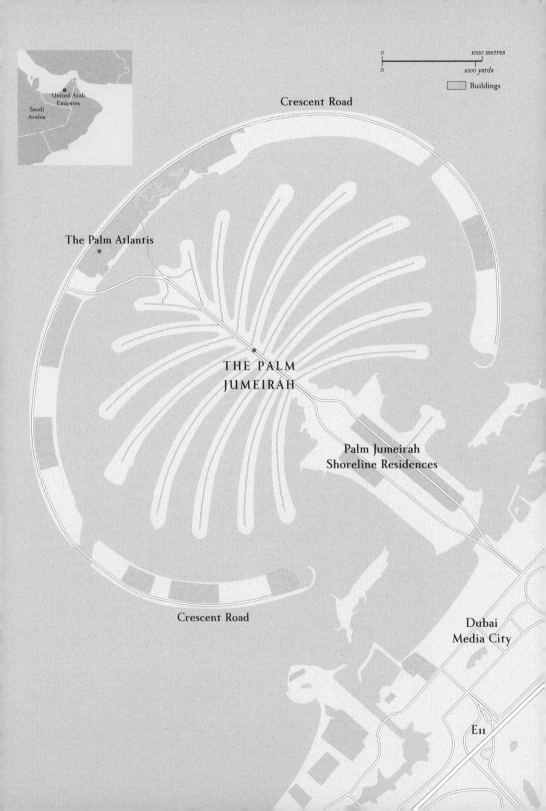

Crescent Road

1000 metres
1000 yards
Buildings

United Arab
Emirates
Saudi
Arabia

The Palm Atlantis

THE PALM
JUMEIRAH

Palm Jumeirah
Shoreline Residences

Crescent Road

Dubai
Media City

E11

The Kingdom of Redonda

Uninhabited Caribbean island

Leeward Islands [Caribbean]

16° 56' 18" N
62° 20' 43" W

Like the bohemia once relished by painters, poets and writers, the Kingdom of Redonda might be said to be a state of the imagination rather than an actual principality. The place itself is real enough, however. Redonda lies some 15 miles north-west of Montserrat, among the Leeward Islands in the Caribbean Sea. Known as Ocanmanru by the native Caribs, it was renamed Santa María la Redonda (St Mary the Round) in recognition of its cone-like shape by Christopher Columbus, who sailed past it on his second voyage of discovery in November 1493.

Reduced to about a third of its size by earthquakes in the late seventeenth century, it was – and still is – a largely unprepossessing, inhospitable slab of volcanic rock. Rising out of the ocean to a height of 975 feet, Redonda is just a mile and half long and almost as bare as a pebble. Its only inhabitants until the nineteenth century were iguanas, small gannets and the herds of goats imported by Montserrat farmers and left to fatten themselves up on the island's sparse vegetation before slaughter. The isle was considered so unimportant that no one bothered to stake an official claim to it. That was all to change after a visit by a group of geologists in the early 1860s. They found Redonda was rich in mineral ores containing high levels of phosphates, which were used in fertilizers. When news of this discovery reached Montserrat, a local sea trader, Matthew Dowdy Shiell, hoping to exploit these natural resources, organized an expedition to seize the island as his personal fiefdom. Landing on 21 July 1865, Shiell was disappointed to meet a team of Americans already busy excavating the phosphate rock. This didn't, however, prevent the Montserrat man from declaring himself

Fulton Peak

King Juan's
Peak

▲ 298 m
971 ft

•

REDONDA ISLAND

Cuba

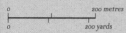

the King of Redonda, a title he duly passed on to his son, Matthew Phipps Shiell, on the boy's fifteenth birthday in 1880. But in the intervening years, the British government, unhappy about American incursions into their colonial territory, had annexed Redonda for themselves. In the ensuing legal wrangle following this intervention into Redondan affairs, the Shiells were eventually to be granted the rights to the regal title but not the island itself: kingship without a kingdom, essentially.

The young Matthew Phipps Shiell was seemingly an imaginative child and from an early age showed a tremendous aptitude with words. This was to lead him into the world of journalism and to London, where, alongside filing reports for *Messenger* newspaper, he began writing fantastical stories for periodicals like *The Strand* and *Pall Mall*. He also lopped the second 'l' off of his surname and styled himself M.P. Shiel. His literary breakthrough came with the creation of a detective to rival Conan Doyle's Sherlock Holmes. Prince Zaleski was an outlandish blue-blooded mystic, whose powers of deduction were so advanced that he didn't even need to visit the scene of a crime. Zaleski's adventures proved popular enough for Shiel

Below: Redonda, the rock from which a semi-fictional royal dynasty has been hewn.

to move into novels. His most celebrated book, *The Purple Cloud*, was an apocalyptic work of science fiction praised by H. G. Wells and a bestseller in 1901.

Shiel's finances, nevertheless, were consistently shaky, and he kept up a punishing schedule of two books a year to stave off penury. The stranger than fiction story of Redonda stayed a largely private matter until later in life when he became acquainted with a bibulous young poet, John Gawsworth.

For a time editor of *Poetry Review*, Gawsworth was to enjoy a Grub Street existence even more impoverished than Shiel's. But in 1936, the elder man of letters, lacking a legitimate heir, named Gawsworth as his Redondan successor and literary executor. The arrangement between the two men was sealed with a mingling of blood, right wrists nicked by a penknife and rubbed together, and an impromptu agreement drawn up on a sheet of monographed notepaper and signed in Shiel's Sussex home. The succession agreed, the task of extending the Redondan peerage was also to begin in earnest with literary friends such as the writers Lawrence Durrell, Henry Miller, Arthur Ransome and poet Edith Sitwell made Dukes and Duchesses of the Realm.

This practice of bestowing honours was to become a persistent feature of Gawsworth's tenure as King Juan of Redonda after Shiel's death in 1947. But Gawsworth's own financial situation was to become so precarious that he placed an advertisement in *The Times* on 21 June 1958 offering his 'Caribbean Kingship with Royal prerogative for sale' at 'a thousand guineas'. He received an approach and an advance payment of £50 in good faith from Prince Bertil of Sweden. But Gawsworth was forced to pass on this deal after it emerged that he had already hocked the kingship to settle a debt. In an odd turn of fate, both the purchaser and his only son predeceased Gawsworth, both dying unexpectedly and within a few months of each other. Though now free to appoint a new heir, Gawsworth was by 1968 in dire straits. Homeless and a hopeless alcoholic, he was reduced to sleeping rough in Hyde Park until friends came to his aid. With his death two years later, disputes about who exactly had been entrusted with the crown almost inevitably arose, and linger to this day.

However, since 1997, Redonda has, in the eyes of most of the world, been blessed by the rule of the great Spanish novelist Javier Marías. Marías, who'd previously produced a fictional portrait of Gawsworth, has established a publishing imprint and cultural prize in the realm's name and dished out Redondan honours to the film directors Francis Ford Coppola and Pedro Almodóvar and the novelists A.S. Byatt and William Boyd.

POVEGLIA ISLAND

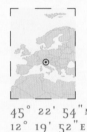

FORMER PLAGUE QUARANTINE ISLAND

VENICE [ITALY]

45° 22' 54" N
12° 19' 52" E

Over the centuries Poveglia, an island five miles off Venice, has had many names. Rich with poplar trees, it was once known as Popilia and was busy and important enough in this region of lagoons to boast its own government in medieval times. But with the advent of the Black Death in the 1340s it acquired a number of sobriquets, including Plague Island and the Isle of Death, which were never likely to make it sound fun or an especially inviting place to live. Indeed, when the plague struck again in the 1500s, Venice's dead and diseased were, according to legend, hauled off to the island and dumped into open pits. The plague-ridden living – men, women and children alike – were either buried or burnt alive with already putrefying corpses. The painter Giorgione, who employed Titian as his assistant, was long thought to have been among the estimated 150,000 plague victims so unceremoniously deposited on Poveglia in this period. More recent evidence appears to indicate, however, that he was more likely to have ended up on another island in the lagoon, Isola del Lazzaretto Nuovo, or the New Island Quarantine. The original lazzaretto was, of course, Poveglia itself. The English word 'quarantine' derives from the Italian quarantina for the forty days anyone showing any signs of illness would be detained on the island before being allowed into Venice, a powerful maritime republic for more than two centuries.

But with the collapse of that republic in 1797 and the migration of naval trade to the ports of Livorno and Trieste, Poveglia was gradually deprived of its once vital role. The island's main church became so ill attended that by the turn of the nineteenth century its bell tower had been turned into

Italy

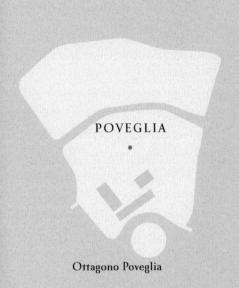

POVEGLIA

Ottagono Poveglia

LAGUNA
VENETA

Lido di
Venezia

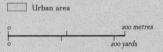

Urban area

0   200 metres
0   200 yards

a lighthouse. In 1922, the old quarantine station was converted into an asylum for the mentally ill and Poveglia gained another new nickname: the Island of Madness. Reputedly the poor inmates were driven further out of their minds by ghosts, the spectres of the unquiet dead from the plague pits. The asylum was finally closed in 1968 and the island has been uninhabited ever since. In the intervening years it has gained an unwelcome reputation for being one of the most haunted places in the world. Some locals refuse to venture onto Poveglia, maintaining that the soil and even the sea surrounding the island is cursed from their contamination with incinerated human remains. Certainly bones can be seen just beneath the surface on many areas of open ground. Dislodged from their shallow

resting places by storm tides, they wash up on its beaches with alarming regularity.

But some of the land is today used for growing crops and vines, and this 18-acre island's years of splendid isolation seem certain to come to an end. In May 2014, the cash-strapped Italian government sold Poveglia at auction for £400,000. The successful bid came from an Italian businessman who has hopes of transforming the asylum into a luxury hotel complex. If he succeeds, it could mean turning the island into a place that the living are dying to visit, rather than a place where only the dying visit, for the first time in nearly 700 years.

GREAT BLASKET

UNINHABITED SINCE 1954

BLASKET ISLANDS [REPUBLIC OF IRELAND]

52° 4' 53" N
10° 34' 5" W

As an island off Ireland, standing some three miles out into the Atlantic to the west of Co. Kerry, Great Blasket is pretty much the only thing standing between its mother country and America – the land to which so many of its poor inhabitants emigrated throughout the nineteenth and twentieth centuries. All of Great Blasket's last twenty-two permanent residents were finally evacuated during 1953 and 1954. With Ireland itself then economically isolated and haemorrhaging its population, the island can almost be seen as a metaphor for, and to an extent a microcosm of, a mainland nation it always stood apart from, geographically and psychologically. Blasket islanders, if admired by mainlanders for their sturdiness and a devotion to a way of life that was as unwaveringly simple as it was grindingly hard, were nevertheless viewed with a certain suspicion by some. Their very separateness – in poor weather the island can sometimes not be reached for days on end – almost inevitably inculcated a degree of insularity that was perhaps off-putting to others.

The remnants of an ancient fort at Dún suggest that Great Blasket was possibly occupied in the Iron Age. However, there is no mention of any inhabitants in a logbook from a ship in the fleeing Spanish Armada of 1588 which stopped off to replenish its supplies of fresh water. The island is generally accepted to have been permanently settled only in the latter half of the seventeenth century. By the census of 1843, the population stood at 153 people living in some twenty-eight dwellings. Throughout its near two-hundred-year existence, the whole community at Blasket lived in a single village of stone houses. This arose on a ridge at the eastern end of the island facing the

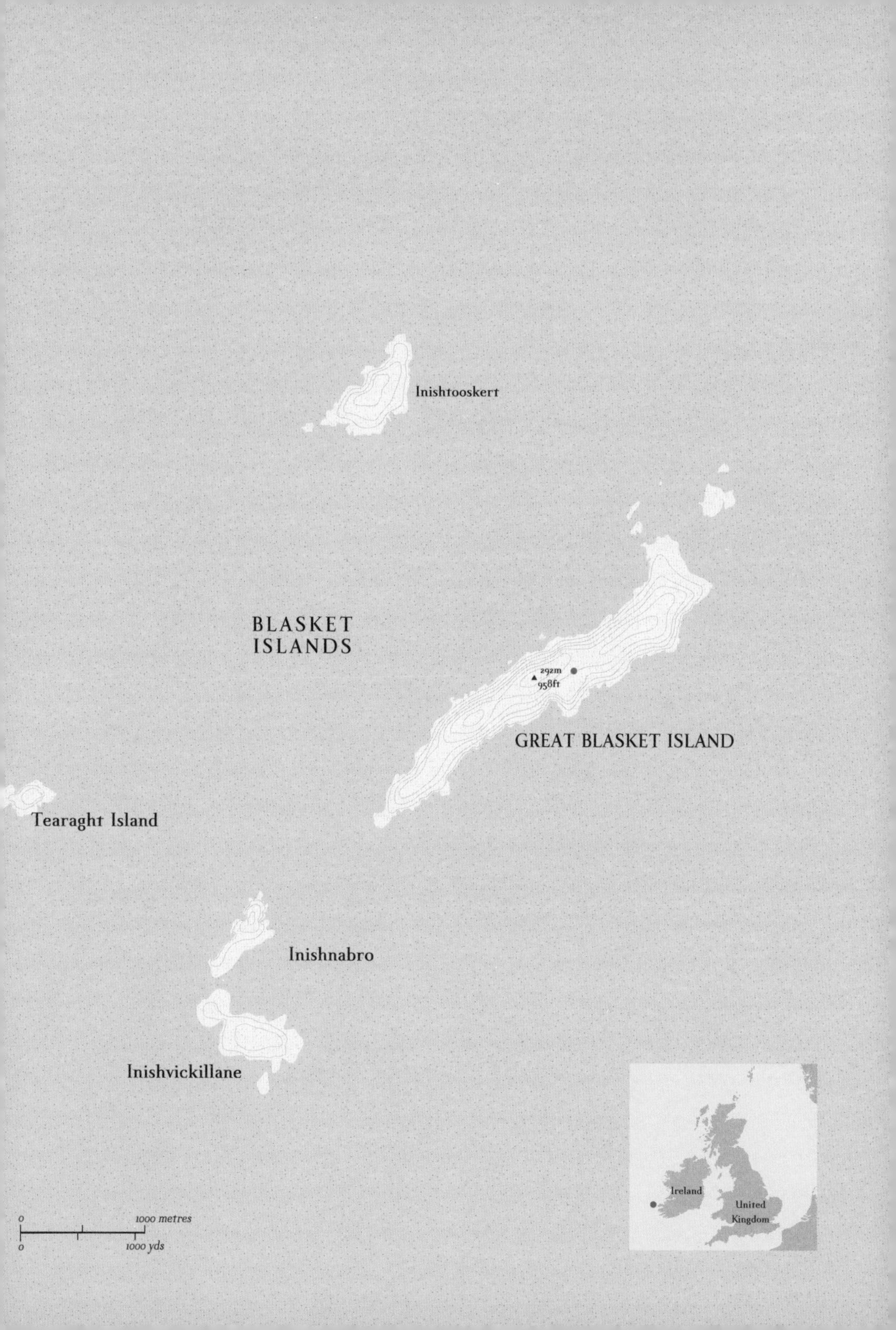

Inishtooskert

BLASKET
ISLANDS

▲ 292m
958ft ●

GREAT BLASKET ISLAND

Tearaght Island

Inishnabro

Inishvickillane

0 _____ 1000 metres
0 _____ 1000 yds

Ireland
United
Kingdom

mainland; the steep hillside here offers at least a smidgen of protection from salty gales whipping in from the Atlantic. And on Blasket salty gales are always whipping in from the Atlantic, a factor that prevents trees, the odd raggedy hebe bushes aside, from prospering here. Other absentees from Blasket, even at its most populous just before the First World War, were a church, a shop, wheeled vehicles and indeed machinery of almost any kind other than hand looms and sewing spindles. Money was used only to trade with the mainland, the islanders themselves doing without it as they did without most other things in an existence based on subsistence farming, fishing for herring and mackerel and the raising and grazing of sheep and cattle. Wool and fish were chief among the island's exports and rowed over in a curragh – or *naomhóg*; they were sold, or bartered and exchanged for bags of meal and sugar, and such rare luxuries as tobacco and porter. Similarly, islanders wishing to receive a Catholic marriage, baptism or burial had to leave Blasket for the bright lights of Dunquin. In the warmer months of the year visiting priests would hold masses in the village school built in 1860 and a Protestant mission also established a short-lived outpost on the island for a time.

Below: Blasket, the last stop before America.

Among themselves, the islanders spoke Gaelic exclusively. English, for the few who had any, was reserved for dealings with the mainlanders. But in the war for independence from Britain and the run-up to the founding of the Irish State in 1922, interest in the Gaelic language and the desire to reconnect with a pre-Anglo-Irish sensibility grew exponentially across the nation. Accordingly, Great Blasket came to be valued as one of the rare repositories of an older, indigenous oral culture. Folklorists, poets, scholars and linguists sought to document Blasket's stories and customs, collecting, translating and publishing works of local history.

Peig Sayers, although born on the mainland, remains the most famous Blasket islander of all. Her autobiography, *Peig*, was for many decades a set text in schools in the Republic, with the result that, alas, the book is less loved than some in the Irish canon. Rather like cross-country running in the rain, school dinners or algebra, her life story, a tale of unrelenting rural hardships borne with faith and the fellowship of other islanders, is widely recalled as something that was endured rather than enjoyed as part of an Irish education. But in her own day, Sayers, who 'married into the island', was revered as a wonderful storyteller and recalled, warmly, as 'a talking machine' by one former Blasket resident. She was herself illiterate, and her books were based on transcripts of reminiscences. Their initial success in the late 1930s and 1940s, in effect, coincided with the demise of that very storytelling tradition and Blasket itself as a sustainable community.

If uninhabited, Great Blasket is no longer entirely without human contact. Today in the high summer as many as 300 people each day catch a ferry over to Blasket, and are conveyed on the final part of that journey by a small dingy to its long sandy shore. Peig Sayers's old home, a white-washed, walled, two-storey property, one of five built in 1910 by the Congested Districts Board to help improve living conditions for the islanders, stands renovated and reborn as a hostel for paying guests. The island, as of 2014, has a café, too. However, Peig herself and Blasket purists might be reassured to learn that running water and electricity continue to be unknown here.

And apart from the tourist season, life on Blasket is arguably wilder than ever. Buck's-horn and pennywort have colonized the gaps in stones of the village's older derelict buildings. Nettles and thistles fill fields once planted with potatoes, and Irish hares, only introduced in the 1990s, dart through the marram grass-infested sand dunes. A quarter of Ireland's entire grey seal population call Blasket home, living, unlike their forebears slaughtered for oil and meat, undisturbed and their habitat under the protection of European law.

Holland Island

Island slowly being eroded by the water
Maryland [United States]

38° 7' 10"N
76° 5' 17"W

A 200-mile-long estuary that runs from Havre de Grace, Maryland, to Norfolk, Virginia, the Chesapeake Bay has often proved treacherous. Countless vessels, from Native American canoes and British tea clippers to iron-clad civil war battleships and contemporary coastal patrol boats, have been wrecked in its waters, which, if for the most part shallow, do have depths of up to 60 feet. But in the last hundred years, rising tides and coastal erosion have had a more devastating effect on parts of Maryland its occupants had previously assumed were good to go as land.

When the English colonist Captain John Smith sailed up the Chesapeake Bay in June 1608, mostly on a desperate hunt for food but also managing to get a decent bit of mapping done, he noted the plethora of islands dotting the bay. One of them was Holland Island. A landmass of 270 acres and some five miles long and six miles offshore, it was settled in the late 1600s by European emigrants, most of whom came from Cornwall in the south-west of England. It was christened after an early resident, Daniel Holland (rather than the north European country famed for its dams and drainage systems), with a name that might now seem almost ironic were it not quite so tragic, for since 2013 Holland Island has all but been under water. Prior to that, however, one man, Stephen White, had fought valiantly, if ultimately to no avail, for nearly twenty years to prevent the island's last standing house and its two remaining graveyards from slipping forever beneath the encroaching waves.

White was far too young ever to have seen Holland Island in its late-Victorian prime. At the turn of the twentieth century, its eastern and

The Last
House on
Holland
Island

*Holland
Island
Bay*

**HOLLAND
ISLAND**

Canda

Washington

United
States

0   200 metres
0   200 yards

western ridgeways were lined with sixty houses and the island's population stood at 360. Among that number were sixty-two children who had the run of a school and a sweetshop. There was a general store, a church with a full-time minister, a doctor and a Red Man's society club house that was the hub of island social life and a baseball team that travelled by barge to games on the mainland. Most of its inhabitants were watermen by trade, the market for the bay's ample stocks of oysters, crabs, clams and sea fowl having grown to encompass the whole country following the extension of the Pennsylvania Railroad to the Tangier Sound fishing town of Crisfield in 1866. The place name Chesapeake itself, incidentally, comes from the Algonquian for 'great shell-fish bay', something Maryland is still famous for today.

But Holland Island's thriving fishing community was built on sand, almost literally in this instance. Like many of the other islands in the bay, it was formed of silt and clay rather than rock. By 1915, the ground was eroding at such an alarming rate that people began to leave the island, most dismantling their clapboard houses piece by piece and shipping them ashore on lighters for reassembly on drier plots around the bay. Within fifteen years the island's only inhabitants were brown pelicans, herons and terns, though its graveyards and few remaining buildings were tended by a visiting caretaker. In the 1940s, when White was a young boy, this job was undertaken by his uncle. White loved to accompany him on his rounds of the island, playing at Robinson Crusoe while his uncle patched up abandoned buildings or collected rubbish and driftwood.

White would grow up and move away and decades would pass before he set foot on Holland Island again. He would work as a Maryland waterman himself before training to be a Methodist minister. On retiring, White bought a boat and in 1989 sailed it to the island he recalled with such fondness from his youth. Landing, he hardly recognized the place and was shaken by just how much had gone – only a single two-storey house dating from the 1880s remained and that was severely weather-beaten. Wandering, slightly dazed by what confronted him, into one of the two waterlogged graveyards, he came upon a broken headstone lying on the ground. On it was carved an epitaph for a girl called Effie Wilson who'd died at just thirteen in 1893. It read: 'Forget me not Is all I ask, I could not ask for more.' Seeing it, White burst into tears and there and then vowed to do everything in his power to preserve Holland Island.

To that end, he lobbied government agencies, bent politicians' ears and eventually purchased the house and the lion's share of the land for $70,000. With his wife Diane, he began to spend nearly every weekend on the island trying to stem the tide. Together they built wooden breakwaters, laid sandbags and placed, by hand, a total of 23 tons of rocks on the shore. But it was never enough, the sea kept coming and in 2003 Hurricane Isabel whipped by, stripping the island of more than half of its trees and weakening the house further. Mocked as the Sisyphus of Dorchester County by some in the press who pointed to statistics which suggested that Maryland was losing 260 acres of tidal shoreline every year, White nevertheless refused to give up. But in 2010 he fell seriously ill, and that October the one remaining house, no longer able to hold out against the elements, collapsed in on itself. Over the following months, the waters of the bay swallowed that up easily enough, and today what little else is left of the island is submerged entirely at high tide.

Below: Holland Island's lone house struggles against the high tides of Chesapeake Bay.

PALMERSTON

A COMMUNITY FORMED IN ITS FOUNDER'S IMAGE
PALMERSTON [COOK ISLANDS]

18° 2' 30"s
163° 8' 48"w

The geographically far-flung Palmerston atoll was first sighted by Captain James Cook and his crew in 1774. The intrepid Yorkshire-born mariner gave it a wide berth on this first encounter but chose in any case (either cannily or obsequiously) to name it after Lord Palmerston, then First Lord of the Admiralty. Returning three years later, and on his third voyage to these South Pacific parts, Cook and co. did indeed venture ashore seeking food and supplies, thus making Palmerston the only single island in the coral reef-bound Cook Islands actually to be graced by a visit of the great man himself.

The island was then uninhabited but in earlier times it had experienced brief periods of native occupation and was already known to the Polynesians as Ava Rau – which translates as something like the Place of 200 Channels. But one name really dominates Palmerston, that of William Marsters. At the last reported count, all but three of the present residents of the island are direct descendants of Marsters. To call Palmerston a close-knit community is an understatement to say the least. It is also an exceedingly small one: today the population stands at just over sixty, down from about 300 in the 1950s and 1960s. Marsters, however, did get the place off to a running start by fathering twenty-three children with his three Maori wives. Hailing from Gloucestershire (or by some accounts Leicester), this English carpenter and cooper had wound up on Manuae Atoll, near Aitutaki after sailing across the Pacific from California, where he'd headed in search of gold in the rush of the 1840s. Clearly a man given to taking a punt on a hunch, he accepted the position of caretaker of the island

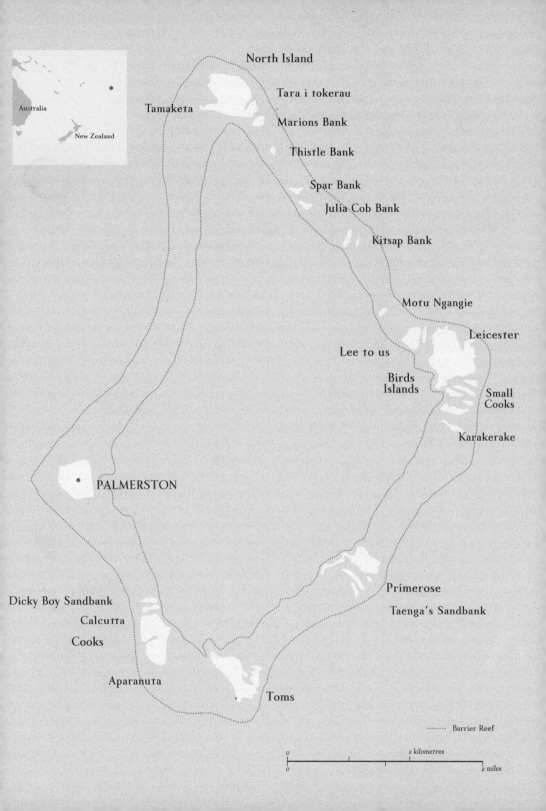

North Island

Tara i tokerau

Tamaketa

Marions Bank

Thistle Bank

Spar Bank

Julia Cob Bank

Kitsap Bank

Motu Ngangie

Leicester

Lee to us

Birds
Islands

Small
Cooks

Karakerake

PALMERSTON

Primerose

Taenga's Sandbank

Dicky Boy Sandbank

Calcutta

Cooks

Aparanuta

Toms

Australia

New Zealand

Barrier Reef

0   2 kilometres

0   2 miles

and sailed the 228 miles to it in 1863 with his first two wives. The third was acquired a short while later, and maybe even a fourth, too. Once on Palmerston, he procreated, hunted the bosun bird, fished for parrot fish (still a prized local delicacy and the island's chief export) and planted palm trees to produce coconut oil and gathered sea cucumbers from the lagoon. The house he built from the timber of shipwrecks still stands today and it was the only structure on the island to escape an appalling hurricane that swept everything else away in 1926.

After a long tussle with the British government, Marsters was eventually granted possession of the island by Queen Victoria in 1892 but died of malnutrition only seven years later after his coconut trees died of blight. Technically administered by New Zealand, Palmerston has its own government and Marsters's descendants were granted full ownership of the island in 1954. Only their relatives are allowed to reside on the island.

What they have, certainly aesthetically, is as close to a Pacific island paradise as you can get – hurricanes aside. Accessible only by boat and by a treacherous approach, this is a place of white sandy beaches, verdant palm trees and pandanus (a palm-like tree) and an abundance of coconut, taro and breadfruit, all surrounded by a clear sea and a lagoon so plentiful with seafood that it serves as a kind of offshore kitchen, to be raided as

the appetite demands. That said, the numbers of parrot fish have dwindled so much in the last twenty years that intermittent bans have had to be imposed to help numbers recover.

The islanders take pride in the peace of their surroundings and the gentility and order of their society. Marsters was apparently quite a severe and devout individual who schooled his offspring in Christian worship. The church continues to be the centre of island life, and barter and exchange remain the main form of custom between islanders themselves. There are no shops, no hotels, no restaurants. Drinking water is chiefly derived from rainwater and plumbing is primitive to non-existent: there are two toilets on the island. An ice-cold beer, nevertheless, can be acquired in the yacht club – but not on Sundays or when stocks run dry. Their main freighter supply ship visits just twice a year, also bringing with it rice and similar staples to be traded for frozen parrot fish and other island produce. Slightly less isolated from the modern outside than it once was, Palmerston is on the internet. And electricity, previously rationed, is now available twenty-four hours a day, thanks to the installation of new solar panels in 2015. Home to the highest number of deep freezers per capita in the entire world, the island especially welcomed this innovation, its people fed up with losing the contents of their freezers whenever the power failed.

Wrangel Island

A place frozen in time
Wrangel [Arctic Ocean, Russia]

71° 14' 55" N
179° 58' 44" W

About 12,000 years ago, rising sea levels caused Wrangel Island to separate from mainland Siberia. Its present location is some 88 miles off the north-eastern coast but back then a few herds of woolly mammoths were also carried away with this drifting landmass. These majestic beasts, close cousins of the elephant, with immense curved tusks and trunks, had first emerged on the Siberian steppes in the middle Pleistocene period, more than 400,000 years earlier. From there these hardy creatures, highly adapted to icy conditions (even their ears were fur-lined), had spread across to North America and Eurasia.

What these particular mammoths were not to know was that Wrangel was to act as a life raft for their species: a sort of Noah's Ark for one type of animal, say, rather than two of every single breed. Over the next 6,000 years or so, while the Wrangel mammoths went about their business on their new island home, their kin elsewhere rapidly began to die out.

No one quite knows why this happened, but some scientists have suggested that climate change depleted the mineral-rich tundra grassland on which these herbivores depended. At the same time, prehistoric man was occupying larger parts of a less icy earth and correspondingly hunting mammoths in ever greater numbers, too. The unholy alliance of these two developments, especially, but combined with others factors, duly expedited the extinction of these creatures along with similar megafauna.

On Wrangel Island, however, and perhaps impervious to the sorties of hunter-gatherers and with just enough edible vegetation, this isolated colony of mammoths succeeded in staving off their own extinction for

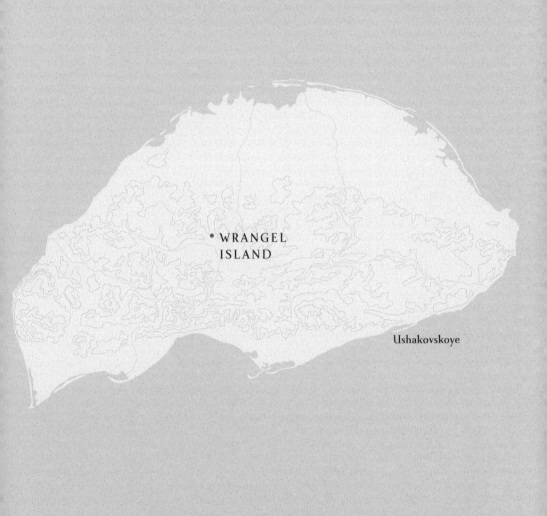

WRANGEL
ISLAND

Ushakovskoye

Russia

Alaska

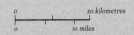

0   20 kilometres

0   10 miles

a good 4,000 years. In 2015, British and Swedish researchers who'd been studying frozen remains there announced that Wrangel's last mammoths probably went in 1650 BC, which, in the scheme of things, is astonishingly recent. The Pyramids in Giza were already a thousand years old by that point.

Since the passing of the mammoths, Wrangel Island has served as a haven for a huge variety of other animals, many of them every bit as threatened by man and changes to the environment as their mammoth predecessors were. The list of wildlife that lives on, or pays seasonal visits to, this most inhospitable of places – an island roughly the size of the US state of Delaware, where the sun does not shine from late November to late February and that is menaced by winds of 90 mph and covered in snow on average 240 days a year – is quite staggering. The roll call includes Pacific walruses, the only nesting snow geese in Asia, musk oxen, Arctic foxes, reindeer, lemmings, and other seabirds and polar bears.

Human beings, on the other hand, have struggled to make much headway on Wrangel. Its remoteness rendered it little more than a rumour for centuries and it continues to be one of the least frequented places on the planet. The Baltic German explorer Ferdinand von Wrangel, who gave the island its name, and ventured out to find it on a wink and a nudge from local Chukchi hunters in the 1820s, never reached it himself. Plenty of others tried and most, as far as can be ascertained, failed. But in 1881 a party from the American steamer *Thomas L. Corwin* successfully landed on Wrangel, hailing it as New Columbia and claiming it for the United States. In 1916, however, Imperial Russia added it to her dominions seemingly unopposed. And although a group of Canadian adventurers did attempt to reclaim it for North America in the 1920s, it has stayed, technically, in Russian hands. Since 1976, the bulk of the island has been classed as a federally managed nature sanctuary. And though the Soviet Union might have ceased to exist, conservation remains the watchword here in one of the world's most remote but (happily) protected wildernesses.

MOUNT RORAIMA

THE LOST WORLD

CANAIMA NATIONAL PARK [VENEZUELA]

5° 8' 31" N
60° 45' 34" W

M ount Roraima is one big story. A mist-wreathed, table-top mountain on the borders of Venezuela, Brazil and Guyana, it was made internationally famous by a novel but was the stuff of travellers' tall tales, explorers' yarns and local myth and legend long before that. Perhaps the greatest compliment that can be paid to it is to say that the human imagination seems almost dwarfed by its reality. Its wonder is that it continues to be a wonder despite being somewhat less mysterious than it once was. These days between 3,000 and 4,000 visitors trek to its summit each year, up from only a few hundred a decade or so ago. Such numbers, while a boon to the Venezuelan economy, are now a growing concern to environmentalists and to the indigenous Pemón people, too.

For the Pemón, who have inhabited the Gran Sabana plateau for centuries, Roraima is a sacred place, one of a chain of mountains across south-eastern Venezuela they know as *tepuis*, or 'houses of the gods'. According to their ancient cosmology, Roraima is believed by the Pemón to be the stump of a mighty tree that bore all the fruits and vegetables of the world. This was felled by mythical trickster called Makunaima, who unleashed a flood and scattered its bounty about the earth. The stump was then turned into stone, at which point it was deemed a suitably lofty, and pleasingly level, perch for the gods to enjoy. Fearing reprisals from these immortals, the Pemón themselves avoided venturing up to its peak. Their reluctance was further reinforced by rumours that the gods, canny real estate agents that they were as well as hard-to-appease deities, had sublet parts of the mountain to a vicious race of apemen.

GUYANA

Tepui Wei-Assipu

BRAZIL

Punto Triple

2200 m
2000 m
1900 m
1800 m
1700 m
1600 m
1500 m
1400 m

2810 m
9220 ft ●◢ Mount Roraima

1300 m

1200 m

1200 m

VENEZUELA

Venezula   Guyana

Brazil

0   5 kilometres

0   3 miles

The first the English-speaking world got to hear about Roraima – and at the time that world was pretty much England and a couple of huts in Virginia – was when Sir Walter Raleigh undertook his journey up the Orinoco to find the fabled city of gold, El Dorado. In the account of this voyage Raleigh published in 1596, he wrote of being told of a 'mountain of crystal' that he later glimpsed from 'afar off' and which 'appeared like a white church-tower of an exceeding height'. A fuller account of Roraima would have to wait until 1838. It was then that the German-born explorer and scientist Robert Schomburgk undertook an expedition of the region on behalf of Britain's Royal Geographical Society. And science as much as mountaineering glory was behind the first successful European assault on its summit by the British botanist and colonial officer Sir Everard im Thurn with the surveyor Harry Perkins in 1884. The specimens im Thurn collected from Roraima and the surrounding area led to the identification

of fifty-three new species by scientists at Kew Gardens. Im Thurn's travels were to inspire Sir Arthur Conan Doyle, creator of Sherlock Holmes, to write *The Lost World*. And although Conan Doyle never set foot on Roraima, this 1912 novel, and the several blockbuster Hollywood film versions of it, is still largely the reason so many head for it today.

Conan Doyle's book imagined Roraima as a realm out of time, a place where dinosaurs and other prehistoric creatures and plants lived on, undisturbed by the steam engine or electricity. If the real Roraima is lacking (perhaps fortunately) velociraptors or stegosauruses, its summit, standing more than 9,200 feet above sea level and ridged by 400-foot cliffs, is inhabited by breeds of black frogs, dragonflies and tarantulas that are found nowhere else on earth.

Below: The roof of Mount Roraima, where Conan Doyle dreamt dinosaurs could still roam.

ROSS ISLAND

BRITISH INDIAN PENAL SETTLEMENT
ANDAMAN ARCHIPELAGO [INDIA]

11° 40' 36" N
92° 45' 41" E

Geographically and climatically closer to Indonesia and Myanmar than the Indian mainland to which they belong, the Andamans are an archipelago of 300 islands in the Bay of Bengal which were occupied by the British for close to a century. Populated by indigenous Sentinelese tribes and Negrito ethnic settlers for more than 2,000 years, they first caught the eye of the British in the 1780s when they were surveyed for the British East India Company by Lieutenant Archibald Blair, who also established a short-lived settlement on South Andaman Island. This was later named Port Blair in his honour, when, in the wake of the First War of Independence (or the Indian Mutiny as it was once known) in 1857, the British decided to build a penal colony on the island. Over the course of its lengthy existence, thousands of Indian freedom fighters would be dispatched to this distant locale. Here they were forced to clear the jungle and to construct the harbour and houses along with prisons for themselves. The latter culminated in the creation at the end of the nineteenth century of one of the most loathed symbols of British oppression: the Cellular Jail. A vast, high-security prison built along the lines of Jeremy Bentham's panopticon, it was known as Kala Pani, or black water, a bitter reference to both the mists that seemed to drift in from the bay, seeping into the prison walls, and the vast expanse of ocean that stood between them and the homeland they were trying to liberate.

While their political prisoners languished on Port Blair, confined in damp, chilly cells, the British who administered the colony lived in some high style on a separate island a mile or so to the east. Ross Island is tiny,

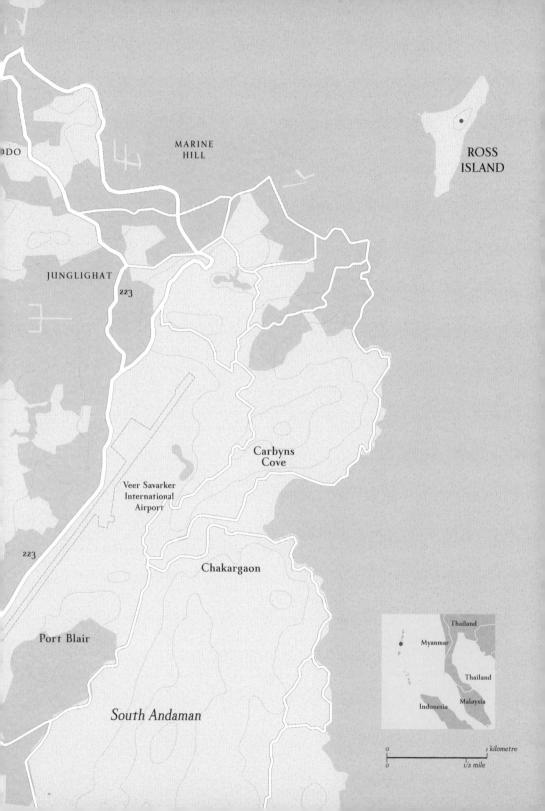

ODO

MARINE
HILL

ROSS
ISLAND

JUNGLIGHAT

223

Carbyns
Cove

Veer Savarker
International
Airport

Chakargaon

223

Port Blair

South Andaman

Thailand

Myanmar

Thailand

Malaysia

Indonesia

| 0 | | 1 kilometre |

| 0 | | 1/2 mile |

just over half a mile square, but it was equipped with everything an English imperialist of the period could possibly wish for. The Chief Commissar's House alone was an extraordinary vast wood-beamed building, with carved gables, whose design owed as much to a Swiss chalet as a house in the Home Counties. Also on the island was an officers' club, a ballroom, hospital, tennis courts, a swimming pool, a church whose teak-framed windows were filled with fine Italian stained glass, a bakery, a water-treatment plant, printers and an ice-making factory. Curiously for such an exclusively British enclave, many of the buildings mainly looked to France for their architectural inspiration, and accordingly Ross was said to be referred to as 'the Paris of the East' by some of its residents. But this cosy little world was shattered, and perhaps with it the illusion of imperviousness, on 26 June 1941, when a series of earthquakes shook the Indian Ocean for three minutes. The Andaman and Nicobar islands were two of the worst affected areas in British India. On Ross, the ballroom floor was split in two, tree roots burst up through the tennis court and most of the houses were left listing badly, more Leaning Tower of Pisa than Paris. Over the bay, ironically, the Cellular Jail stood completely unharmed.

In less than a year, however, the Andamans were overrun by the Japanese, who added concrete bunkers to the islands' quota of architectural oddities. After the Second World War, Ross was briefly reoccupied by the British but abandoned soon afterwards. Its buildings have since fallen into ever more advanced, and perhaps more aesthetic, forms of ruin, their wrecked tiled floors and verandas teeming with tropical vegetation. Now officially in the hands of the Indian navy, and claimed by spotted deer and peacocks, Ross stands as a decayed relic of the Raj, its ruins a pleasant reminder to many modern Indians that the worst of those days are long gone now.

HIRTA

THE EDGE OF THE WORLD
ISLE OF ST KILDA [SCOTLAND]

57° 48' 48" N
8° 35' 7" W

The St Kilda archipelago, of which Hirta is the largest island, was once the British Isles' remotest inhabited outpost. The medieval scribe John of Fordun described it as being 'on the margine of the world', while King James IV of Scotland thought the islands too remote to bother including within his kingdom. A boat from the Scottish mainland can still take up to eighteen hours to reach it. Even the Western Isles (its closest neighbours are the Uists) are a three- to six-hour trip away. Journeys to St Kilda are at the mercy of Outer Hebridean weather not famed for its clemency. The islands receive on average 50 inches of rain a year but are subject to ferocious storms and gales between September and March. Mary Cameron, the daughter of one of Hirta's last ministers, recalled one storm that was so severe it left the islanders deaf for a week. The noise of the howling wind and the pounding of the heavy seas, she maintained, actually drowned out the sound of the thunder and lightning. But lying in the path of the Gulf Stream, St Kilda has winters that are less chilly than might be expected and its springs and summers can be humid and sunny. On bright, windless days, Hirta, lacking any trees to offer shade, can even get quite hot: hot enough for male St Kildans of old to be recorded digging their plots stripped to the waist on occasions when the noonday sun was at its strongest.

Essentially the remains of a volcano that erupted some fifty to sixty million years ago, this apparently inhospitable archipelago has known human life since prehistoric times. Its inhabitants, like the occupants of the Outer Hebrides, were crofters, who dug peat, grew crops, kept cattle and

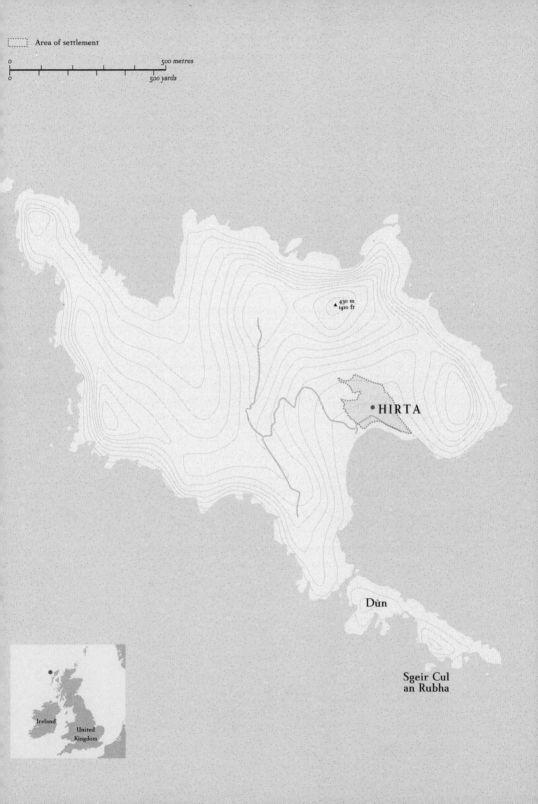

Area of settlement

0   500 metres

0   500 yards

▲ 430 m
  1410 ft

•HIRTA

Dùn

Sgeir Cul
an Rubha

Ireland

United
Kingdom

raised Soray sheep for meat, milk and wool for weaving. But the isolation
of their home and its particular topography created a uniquely individual
community. While taking what they could from the treacherous waters
around them, the islanders made not fish but seabirds their staples: the
gannets, petrels, puffins and fulmars which thrive around St Kilda. The
cliffs that surround Hirta are the highest in Britain, their ledges, nooks and
crevices making a perfect environment for nesting seabirds. Almost entirely
self-sufficient until the nineteenth century, the Gaelic-speaking islanders
paid their rent in kind for generations and would spend eight months of
each year entirely cut off from the outside world. As late as 1909, St Kilda

was operating on the Old Style Calendar, and toasting in the New Year on 12 January rather than 1 January.

If fiercely proud of their independence, the population gradually became more dependent on imports of coal and the like to heat their homes. The numbers of inhabitants also started to dwindle. There were outbreaks of disease: sightseers on charter tours designed to supply urban types with glimpses of a simpler, unchanging life, brought with them some common ailments that proved fatal here. The allure of a new life in a new world called younger islanders to Australia, and a suburb of Melbourne named St Kilda is testament to this exodus. By 1930 there were only thirty-six islanders left and, concluding that their timeless way of life was no longer tenable, they asked to be evacuated and rehoused on the mainland. The story of their departure was the subject of a 1937 film by Michael Powell entitled *The Edge of the World*. It was filmed on Foula in the Shetlands and, though somewhat melodramatic, its innovative use of period locations and employment of local people gives a real idea of just how traumatic the withdrawal must have been for St Kildans at the time.

In the hands of the National Trust for Scotland since 1957, St Kilda has not been left to the birds; today it is even occupied for brief parts of the year by Trust staff and natural scientists undertaking research. From April to September, day trippers come to marvel at what once was, its wildlife and its dramatic scenery: around the islands are giant rock formations called stacks, which loom as menacingly as icebergs out of the surrounding ocean.

Left: The abandoned island of St Kilda. The timeless way of life once enjoyed on the isle is no longer possible in today's world.

OTHERWORLDLY SPACES

AOKIGAHARA

THE DEMON FOREST
MOUNT FUJI [JAPAN]

35° 27' 45.3" N
138° 39' 15.8 E

Forests are the stuff of fairy tales, usually a wee bit dangerous, and inhabited by big bad wolves and mischievous boggarts but for the most part more enchanted than evil, if slightly menacing. Aokigahara, located in the foothills of Japan's Mount Fuji, on the other hand, is another proposition entirely.

A sign at the entrance to the forest urges those entering to consider their families. As well it might, for Aokigahara is the world's second most popular spot for committing suicide, edged into second place only by the Golden Gate Bridge in San Francisco.

Between fifty and a hundred bodies are reclaimed every year from its exceedingly dense thickets of evergreen trees and amid its woody vines and rocky enclaves. Some of them may well have lain undiscovered for years. This forest is a creepy and deeply unforgiving place. Known alternatively as the 'Sea of Trees', 'Demon Forest' and, indeed, 'Suicide Forest', Aokigahara is treacherous enough already for those with only self-preservation on their mind. The forest floor is uneven and there is no shortage of potentially lethal exposed roots, bent coppices, crevices and hidden caves to negotiate. Navigation, even in these supposedly switched-on times, is further hindered by deposits of magnetic iron in the forest's soil which interfere with compasses, mobile phone signals and GPS systems.

Sadly, self-destruction is more usually the reason people venture into Aokigahara, though its topography is such that it frequently claims the indecisive or uncertain. Why exactly the suicidal come to Aokigahara is a matter for debate. A novel by Seicho Matsumoto entitled *Kuroi*

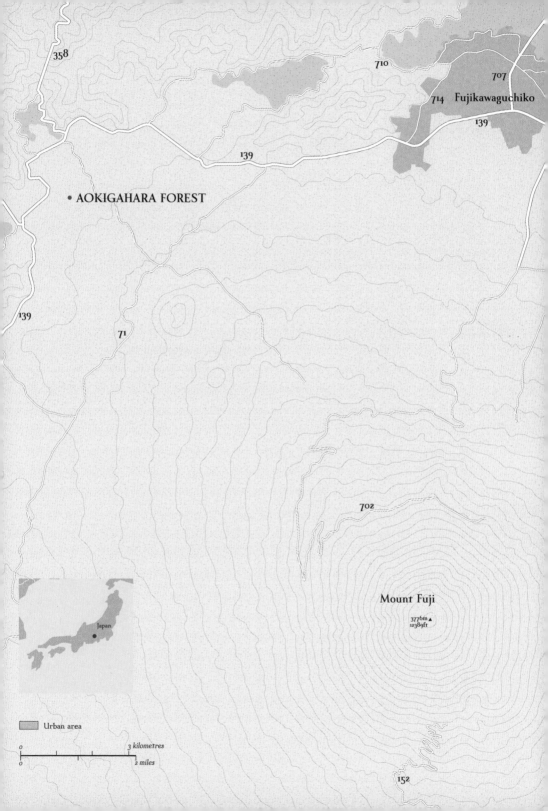

358

7¹⁰

7⁰⁷

7¹⁴ Fujikawaguchiko

139

139

• AOKIGAHARA FOREST

139

7¹

7⁰²

Japan

Mount Fuji

3776m ▲
12389ft

Urban area

0   3 kilometres

0   2 miles

152

Jukai (*Black Sea of Trees*) and published in 1960, which concludes with two lovers committing suicide in the forest, has been condemned for initiating the contemporary Aokigahara death cult. But history suggests the phenomenon existed long before that and in earlier times of impoverishment, weaker children, the sick and the elderly were shunted into the forest and left to almost certain death to reduce the burden on their families. And their ghosts, according to local mythology, have been inviting others to join them in the afterlife ever since.

Suicide in Japan was once the preserve of the elite Samurai. *Seppuku* (or *harakiri*) was a highly ritualized form of self-disembowelment, committed to preserve their honour or to avoid being tortured or executed by their enemies. That 'noble' heritage partially explains the alarmingly high rate of suicide that persists in the country to this day.

Left: The treacherous trees of Aokigahara.

COLMA

CITY OF THE DEAD
CALIFORNIA [UNITED STATES]

37° 40' 16"N
122° 26' 40"W

'It's great to be alive in Colma!' runs the official slogan for this small town in San Mateo County, about ten miles south of San Francisco. There is perhaps a hint of irony in this slogan, for in Colma the living are a rare minority group, numbering only about 1,400. The dead, on the other hand, add up to more than a million, and possibly close to two million. They are buried in the seventeen cemeteries – including one for pets – that occupy 73 per cent of this 2.25-square-mile town.

Colma didn't start out as a necropolis. It was settled as a farming community more than one hundred and fifty years ago, founded by prospectors, hardy frontiersmen and women initially lured west by reports of gold in California, who then chose to knuckle down to something more stable with their shovels and pans, here at the base of the San Bruno Mountains. A bigger attraction for most other migrants seeking to make their name, or at least a buck, was San Francisco. By the 1880s, the city was struggling to cope with the influx. With space at a premium, the dead were as much of an issue as the living, as land was becoming too valuable to be used for burials.

In an increasingly densely populated, and perpetually foggy, metropolis, there were also worries about the healthiness of living in such close proximity to this city's existing and overcrowded graveyards. Spelling out its anxieties in a rather alarmist editorial in May 1887, the *San Francisco Newsletter and California Advertiser* newspaper stated:

The objection to living near a cemetery is no mere sentiment . . .
Half a million pounds of putridity are annually boxed up and

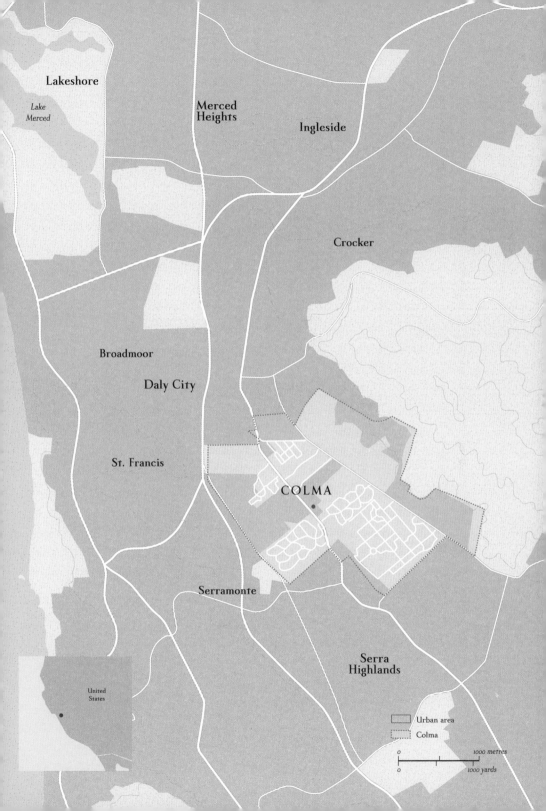

Lakeshore

Lake Merced

Merced Heights

Ingleside

Crocker

Broadmoor

Daly City

St. Francis

COLMA

Serramonte

Serra Highlands

United States

Urban area

Colma

0   1000 metres
0   1000 yards

covered with a few feet of earth. The scientist knows that all the evils
of this decomposition are but disguised by stone vaults and costly
cerements. The germs of disease grow and are diffused in spite of
them. They rise to the surface from the deepest grave to poison both
the earth and the air. They descend to contaminate the springs of
water; years do not destroy them. Putrefaction is actually prolonged
indefinitely and there is continued danger to the living whilst the
process lasts.

That same year, and evidently grasping the acuteness of the situation,
San Francisco's Catholic archbishop Patrick Riordan acquired 283 acres
at Colma for use as a burial ground. The congregation of the city's Temple
Emanu-El followed suit, buying land at Colma for a Jewish cemetery in
the following year, 1888. After the city fathers moved to ban all burials
within its limits in 1890, Colma soon became the only place in town – or
more accurately and quite specifically *outside* town – for San Franciscans
to be interred. Colma's cemeteries, which quickly multiplied to satisfy the
demands of the Bay Area's diverse ethnic and denominational mix, received
a further boost in 1912, when the San Francisco Board of Supervisors
ordered the disinterment and removal of all the bodies buried in the city.
That eviction would take the best part of thirty years and see thousands
upon thousands of remains carried, first by horse-drawn hearses and later
daily funeral street cars, from San Francisco to Colma for reinterment.
Archbishop Riordan's Catholic Holy Cross Cemetery, Colma's first and
still its largest, received some 39,307 bodies alone. Not all of those remains
could be identified after decades in the ground, and unknowns had to be
reburied in mass graves. Colma's Japanese Cemetery, established in 1901,
has a memorial marking a plot that contains 107 bodies moved here from
their earlier resting places at Laurel Hill in San Francisco.

In addition, Colma holds some of America's more dearly remembered.
The San Francisco Seals and New York Yankees baseball star Joe DiMaggio,
who was briefly married to Marilyn Monroe, lies in Holy Cross. Levi Strauss,
the pioneering manufacturer of blue jeans, rests in the Home of Peace, and
the megalomaniac newspaper magnate William Randolph Hearst in the
Cypress Lawns Memorial Park. Bill Graham, the rock music impresario
closely associated with such San Francisco bands as the Grateful Dead
and Jefferson Airplane, is in Eternal Home. And Wyatt Earp, the lawman
famously associated with the gunfight at the OK Corral in Tombstone,
Arizona, in 1881 lies in Hills of Eternity. His own original tombstone, a
250-pound marker in concrete, was stolen in 1957.

LEAP CASTLE

THE WORLD'S MOST HAUNTED RESIDENCE

CO. OFFALY [REPUBLIC OF IRELAND]

53° 1' 41"N
7° 48' 30"W

The poet, critic and prolific author Sacheverell Sitwell professed in 1936 that for him 'no house in the world' held 'so many suggestions of the supernatural' as Leap Castle. Praise indeed coming from Sitwell, the youngest of three famously eccentric, artistic aristocratic siblings whose own Jacobean stately pile, Renishaw Hall in Derbyshire, was notorious for its gloominess and its ghosts.

Leap, pronounced 'Lepp', Castle is perched on a 635-foot-high ridge north of Roscrea, in Co. Offaly. In the heart of the Irish midlands, it lies on the once strategically important route between Munster and Leinster. Until the country's conquest by Oliver Cromwell's forces in 1649, this entire region of Ireland was dominated by the fearsome O'Carroll clan. If often riven by bitter personal rivalries and engaged in bloody feuds, the O'Carrolls were so powerful that they were referred to as 'the Lords to whom stoop the hazelnut trees'. Ruling this particular district on their behalf in ages past, however, were the O'Bannons, whom local legend credits with providing the castle with its name – and building it, or at least the earliest forerunner in wood, on the same site. At some time in the past, according to a story still tirelessly told by the loquacious in the cosy pubs of neighbouring Birr and Kinnitty, two O'Bannon brothers were locked in a dispute about who should inherit the castle and its lands. For reasons that from a twenty-first-century perspective appear opaque or merely insane, they opted to settle this matter by jumping off a crag. The one who survived the fall essentially got the castle. Presumably one of them did – though, of course, both of them might just as likely have perished. Or been left in such

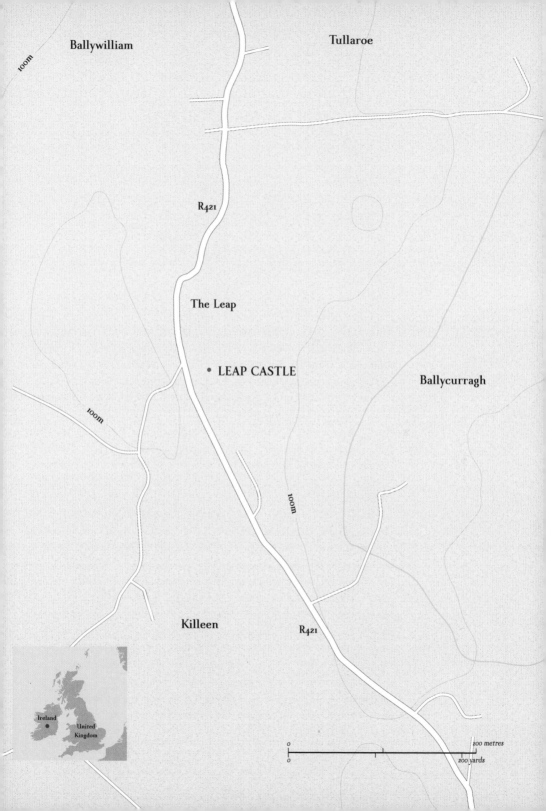

Ballywilliam

Tullaroe

100m

R421

The Leap

● LEAP CASTLE

Ballycurragh

100m

100m

Killeen

R421

Ireland

United
Kingdom

0   200 metres
0   200 yards

an appalling physical state that the property was of no real use to either of them. Whatever the outcome, the castle apparently came to be known as Leim-ui-Banain, or O'Bannon's Leap, in tribute to this legacy-defining incident.

The present castle, or what is left of it, dates from the fifteenth century. It is an example of what is called a 'tower house' – a heavily fortified residence – and in places the walls at Leap are 13 feet thick, with the main buildings originally surrounded by a walled courtyard for good measure. In the late eighteenth century and in line with an architectural fashion stirred by the likes of Sir Horace Walpole's castellated mansion Strawberry Hill in Twickenham, south-west London, the castle was given a more antiquated appearance when it underwent a Gothic makeover. By then, the castle had been in the hands of the Darby family for over a century. A beneficiary of Cromwell's post-conquest largesse, Jonathan Darby, an officer in the New Model (Parliamentary) Army, had received the castle in lieu of wages.

A listing in *Traveller's Directory Through Ireland* of 1803 describes Leap as 'a most beautiful seat, and fine castle, with noble and extensive demesnes, plantations and walks, belonging to Mr Darby'. Ghosts, however, are notable here only by their absence. A century later, though, stories about 'unaccountable apparitions' at Leap were legion. The fame of the Leap ghosts spread throughout the world, helped in large part by the then lady of the manor herself, Mildred 'Milly' Darby. Milly wrote numerous articles about her own experience of hauntings, along with occult-flavoured tales for popular magazines. This was much to the chagrin of her irascible husband Jonathan, who refused to countenance any talk of ghosts at Leap, once declaring that the only spirits in his house were in the wine cellar.

But reports by other family members, staff and guests of shadowy forms wandering through the buildings continued nonetheless. Among the figures frequently sighted were a tonsured-monk in a black cowl, a woman in red, two young girls and a stern-looking old man in green. A visiting clergyman was a victim of another noted Leap spectre, one that reputedly liked nothing more than to heave the slumbering out of their beds, depositing them stunned and bruised on the floor and swathed in a jumble of blankets and sheets. On other occasions in this era, strange lights were spotted in the windows of unoccupied wings. A bloodstain appeared and disappeared on the wooden floor of one chamber. Dogs were subject to sudden fits of barking; horses in the castle grounds would unaccountably freeze in their tracks and maids, overwhelmed by intense feelings of dread, refused to enter certain rooms.

Those seeking root causes for these uncanny occurrences pointed to the history of the O'Carrolls. This Irish dynasty's penchant for murdering members of their own family is certainly impressively Shakespearean in terms of treachery and body count to suggest that the dead might be justified in plaguing the living at Leap. Of all the castle's phantoms, though, the most terrifying was something christened 'The Elemental'. Supposedly of a quite hideous appearance, human in shape though 'inhuman in its vileness', this 'thing' was said to have cadaverous, grey rotting flesh, dark holes for eyes, bony claw-like hands and arms covered in coarse black animal hair. In 1922 ordinary life at Leap came to an abrupt end when the castle was doused with petrol and set ablaze by local Irish republican sympathizers.

Though it was left as a burnt-out shell for the next fifty years, its ghosts seemed unconcerned. Throughout those decades, ethereal beings continued to clock in, to the joy of ghost hunters and investigators of psychic phenomena. Repairs were started on the castle in 1970s and since 1991, when the musician Seán Ryan bought it and moved in with his wife Ann Callanan, these visitors from the afterlife have again had to share Leap with representatives from our own more mundane dimension.

Below: More than a few ghosts have claimed this castle.

Darvaza Crater

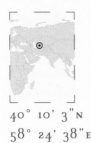

Door to Hell

DARVAZA [TURKMENISTAN]

40° 10' 3"N
58° 24' 38"E

Theologians of various faiths have long wrestled with the concept of hell, pondering for two millennia, if not longer, its supposed location and size, and which sins merit being hurled for all eternity into its predominantly fiery pits – along with what kind of deal the Devil, or some similarly malevolent force, must have struck with their energy supplier to manage those fuel bills. Toasting the damned, after all, doesn't appear to come especially cheap, seemingly requiring flames that 'burn everlasting', and teams of demons, serpents and God knows what else to administer excruciating punishments often, if on a whim, until doomsday.

The Darvaza Crater in the Karakum or Black Sands Desert in Turkmenistan has earned the reputation as the Door to Hell because it has been burning continuously since 1971, according to most, though not all, sources. It was then, or so the well-worn story goes, that Soviet geologists drilling a borehole for natural gas blundered and created a deep sinkhole oozing potentially poisonous methane vapours. Worried that it would contaminate the surrounding area, they set it alight, believing that it would soon extinguish itself. As of 2016, the Door to Hell burns on. Spitting out fearsome angry orange-yellow flames that shimmer in the night sky for miles around and reeking of sulphur, this 225-foot-wide by 99-foot-deep cavern is a picture of a fiery pit straight out of Hieronymus Bosch or Dante Alighieri.

What's more, and emblematic to some of a certain profligacy in a country that has the sixth largest natural gas reserves in the world, the cavern is presently being marketed as a potentially lucrative tourist landmark. The Turkmenistan government hopes that, along with the flora and fauna of

DARVAZA
(DOOR TO HELL)

Kazakhstan

Uzbekistan

Caspian
Sea

Turkmenistan

Iran

0 ——————————— 200 metres
0 ——————————— 200 yards

the surrounding desert, all 220,000 acres of which were declared a state nature reserve in 2014, the Door to Hell will lure tourists to what remains one of the former Soviet Union's most remote and least visited outposts.

That some creatures, worms in particular, appeared to be able to exist and thrive in extremely hot springs was a matter of enormous concern to St

Augustine when this early Christian theologian was musing on the nature of hell. And thanks to a death-defying descent by the Canadian explorer and storm chaser George Kourounis, to the floor of the Darvaza Crater in 2013, we now know from rock samples he collected that life, in the form of bacteria, is present even here, in this seemingly utterly uninhabitable spot, itself located in land few might view as heaven-sent just yet.

THE HILL OF CROSSES

HOME TO SOME 100,000 CROSSES

KRYŽIU KALNAS [LITHUANIA]

56° 0' 55" N
23° 25' 0" E

S imultaneously a symbol of triumph and salvation but also of incredible suffering and an agonizing death, the cross is the universal Christian symbol, embraced by all denominations as an emblem of their faith regardless of any other differences in doctrine. But on a hill some 7½ miles north of the city of Šiauliai, hundreds and thousands of crosses – from the most basic of hand-bound wooden twigs to magnificently carved crucifixes several feet high – stand as a testament to both religious devotion and a lengthy and fraught struggle for Lithuanian nationhood.

The act of planting crosses in the ground of the hill here, little more than a mound 33 feet at its highest point, is typically traced back to the first of several unsuccessful rebellions staged by indigenous Lithuanian peasants against their Russian overlords in 1831. Lacking, in many instances, bodies to bury, people erected crosses to stand as memorials to the missing and small totems of resistance. Though some local historians believe that this tradition could date as far back as the fourteenth century, when Šiauliai was overrun by marauding Teutonic knights, it was fully entrenched by 1900, when at least 130 crosses were recorded standing there.

Granted independence from Russia following the First World War, when the hill became a site of regular prayer meetings, Šiauliai was captured by the Germans in the Second World War and heavily shelled by the Soviet Russian army as they battled to regain it. Thankfully, it was freed from the Nazis, but by 1944 Lithuania had been incorporated into the USSR as the Lithuanian Soviet Socialist Republic. Under Soviet communism, religious observance was forbidden and the Hill of Crosses was declared out of

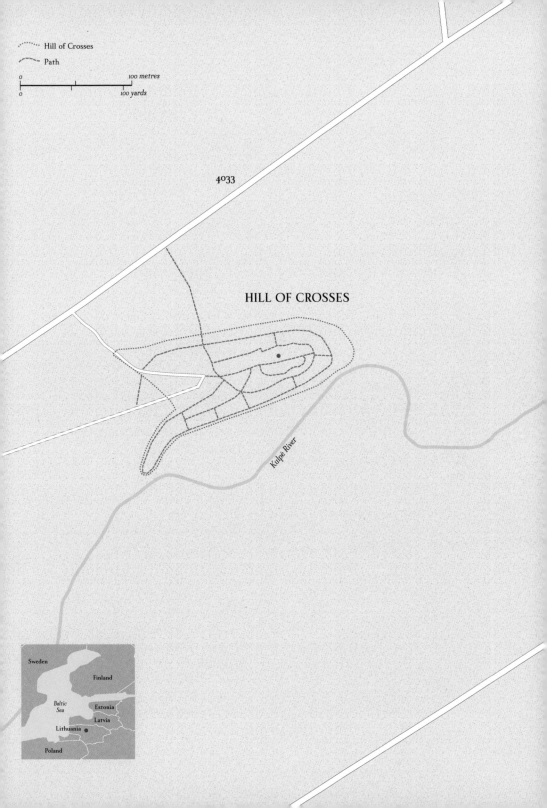

Hill of Crosses ·······
Path — —

0   100 metres
0   100 yards

4°33

HILL OF CROSSES

Kulpė River

Sweden
Finland
Baltic
Sea
Estonia
Latvia
Lithuania
Poland

bounds. Those unwilling or unable to give up the Catholic faith – which 80 per cent of the country's population today still profess to practise – were heavily represented in the quarter of million Lithuanians dispatched to the icy wastes of Siberia and often to premature deaths by Stalin, until the tyrant's own demise in 1953. But the hill only took on a renewed significance as an arena for memorial and dissent. In defiance of cordons and KGB guards, people continued to plant crosses. The authorities responded by sending in the bulldozers on three separate occasions, but new crosses sprang up after each clearance, the total obliteration of all that had stood before and the soiling of the hill with sewage failing to deter the pious and Lithuanian partisans. With the collapse of the Soviet Union in 1991, Lithuania was able once again to enjoy its independence. The Hill of Crosses, revered ever since nationally as a site of immense political and spiritual importance, has grown exponentially and is estimated to include more than 100,000 crosses. Pilgrims come from all corners of the globe, thousands choosing to follow the example set by the Holy Father Pope John Paul II, who planted a cross here himself in 1993.

Left: The hill rendered holy with thousands of crosses.

THE ISLAND OF DOLLS

A TERRIFYING ATTRACTION

XOCHIMILCO [MEXICO]

19° 17' 24"N
99° 5' 38"w

On the outer fringes of Mexico City, some 15 miles away from the centre of this most sprawling of capitals, is Xochimilco – 'the place where flowers grow' or 'the garden of flowers', as the Aztecs called it. Here are the last vestiges of a gigantic and ancient system of canals, terracotta aqueducts and tens of thousands of man-made islands and floating gardens, called *chinampas*, which once stretched across the lagoons of the Valley of Mexico in pre-Conquistador days. The Spaniards called time on this semi-aquatic realm, damming rivers and draining lakes to build roads and bring the Aztec island metropolis of Tenochtitlan closer into line with the likes of Toledo or Seville in the Old World. What they failed to fill in has struggled ever since to fend off advancing urbanization. But at least today what remains of the canals has been afforded World Heritage status and weekend pleasure trips along them can be enjoyed on wooden gondola-like barges called *trajineras*, to the strains of passing waterborne mariachi bands cherished by Chilangos (residents of Mexico City) and tourists alike.

A far more modern addition to Xochimilco's assets, though, is the frankly macabre Isla de las Muñecas, or Island of the Dolls – a destination whose main selling point is its sheer creepiness. On this tiny *chinampa* in the canals hardly a tree is without a doll hanging from it. And most have several strung from their branches on ropes. On the side of a wooden shack, naked Barbie dolls nailed up by their hair compete for wall space with plastic trolls and the raggedest Raggedy Ann cloth dolls ever sewn.

If the dolls' appearance is unsettling, so too is their reason for being there in the first place. It is said that the island's sole inhabitant, a hermit

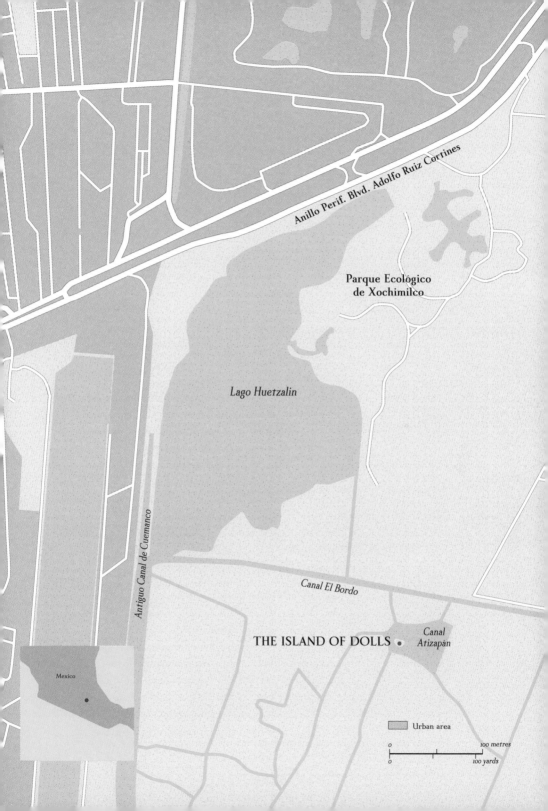

Anillo Perif. Blvd. Adolfo Ruiz Cortines

Parque Ecológico
de Xochimilco

Lago Huetzalin

Antiguo Canal de Cuemanco

Canal El Bordo

THE ISLAND OF DOLLS •   *Canal
Atizapán*

Mexico

Urban area

0   100 metres

0   100 yards

named Don Julian Santana Barrera, came across the body of a small girl who had drowned in the canal one day. The following morning a child's doll floated to the shore at the same spot. Believing that the toy must have belonged to the dead girl, he hung it up in a nearby tree as a memorial to her and a talisman to ward off evil spirits. The arrival of another doll the day after that seems to have turned a one-off tribute into an obsession and before long Don Julian was fishing about in the canal and scouring local rubbish dumps for more dolls to place in trees and to furnish his makeshift abode. After he had accumulated unwanted dolls for some years, news of his doll-bedecked *chinampa* spread, and *trajineras* full of the curious began stopping by his island, some bringing with them dolls as gifts. In 2001, Don Julian died, allegedly drowning in the canal in the very same part of the waterway that claimed the life of the young girl years earlier. Whatever the truth of that, new dolls keep being added to the trees even as the older ones rot away and decay, the life cycles of these anthropomorphic creations proving alarmingly similar to our own.

Left: Some of the thousands of dolls left in tribute to a drowned girl.

SUBTERRANEAN REALMS

The Underground Postal Railway

Rail Mail
London [United Kingdom]

51° 30' 26"N
0° 7' 39"W

As the birthplace of the world's first underground railway – the Metropolitan line from Bishop's Road, Paddington, to Farringdon Street, which opened in 1853 – London has long been a city with hidden depths. Beneath its pavements, there remain plenty of tunnels and pipes ferrying people and/or materials, some less savoury than others, here, there and everywhere. And until 2003, the eager seeker of things subterranean in the British capital could find 6½ miles of tunnel and train track actively dedicated to the transportation of letters and parcels stretching from Paddington in the west to Whitechapel in the East End, once the haunt of Jack the Ripper.

This underground postal railway, known from 1987 as the Rail Mail, was conceived shortly before the First World War. It was planned and built to resolve the problems inherent in distributing post around London's main sorting offices, in the days when roads were clogged by horse-drawn and primitive motor traffic and major parts of the city were all but smothered by impenetrable fog. Finally opening in 1927 (though its uncompleted tunnels were used to store artworks from the Tate Gallery and the National Portrait Gallery a decade earlier during wartime Zeppelin raids), it chalked up another first for London as the world's earliest driverless electric railway. At its height it consisted of eight stations, when letter and sundry other items were taken and delivered several times a day but sadly, its network shrunk to a mere three stations with the advent of the telephone, email and text messaging. Since September 2017 however, the rail mail has reopened as the main attraction at the brand new postal museum in Farringdon.

Overleaf: The previously defunct and empty Rail Mail tunnel, now re-opened as a tourist attraction.

Hampstead
Heath

Regents
Park

MOUNT
PLEASANT

OLD
WESTERN
PARCELS
OFFICE

LIVERPOOL
STREET

ADDINGTON

LONDON WALL

EASTERN
DISTRICT
OFFICE

WESTERN
PARCELS
OFFICE

NEW
WEST
DISTRICT
OFFICE

KING
EDWARD
BUILDING

Bayswater
Road

Hyde
Park

Green
Park

St
James's
Park

River Thames

River Thames

Battersea
Park

Ireland

United
Kingdom

Clapham
Common

● Main postal office

┄┄┄ Unused postal tunnel

0   2 kilometres

0   2 miles

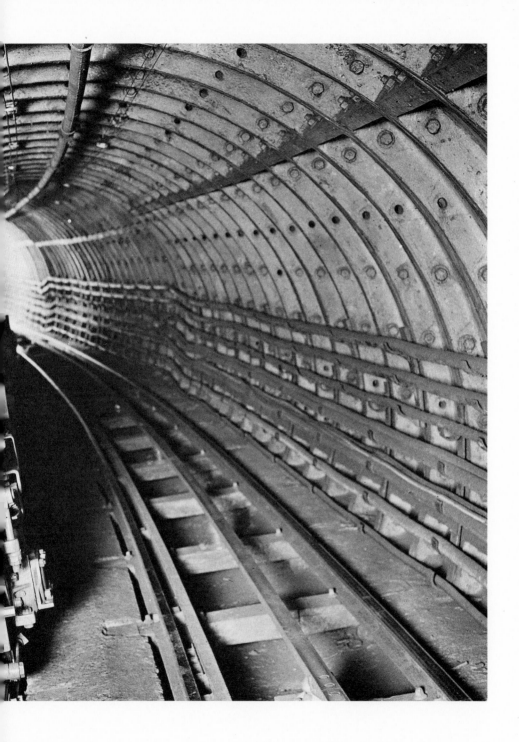

COLD WAR SPY TUNNEL

THE TELEPHONE TAPPING CENTRE
BERLIN [GERMANY]

52° 24' 45" N
13° 31' 40" E

The word 'spy' comes from the Old French *espier*, 'to observe'. But during the Cold War, listening rather than looking seems to have been more important in terms of espionage for both the USSR and the United States and its allies in Western Europe. One of the most audacious and concerted spying campaigns undertaken by the CIA with their British colleagues at MI6 involved tapping the Soviet telephone lines that ran through an East Berlin exchange. This in an age when telephones were attached to sockets in walls, and communication was made possible by electronic currents passing down physical lines. (In those simpler times, a mobile was something you hung in a child's pram, and a cell was a barred and locked room into which criminals or political opponents were dispatched after a confession had been beaten out of them.) To bug these lines, therefore, Anglo-American agents had to dig a 1,476-foot-long tunnel from Rudow in West Berlin to Altglienicke in Soviet-occupied East Berlin in order to install their interception cables.

The project was officially code-named Operation Stopwatch or Operation Gold. Less officially, it was dubbed Harvey's Hole after William Harvey, a big cheese in the CIA in Berlin and a one-time employee of the FBI dismissed by J. Edgar Hoover for drinking on duty. Work on the tunnel began in 1954 and required the mammoth task of moving 3,100 tons of earth. Its construction took several months and cost the Americans $6.7 million, no small sum then. The British supplied the technical equipment, their agents having previously run a similar eavesdropping operation in Vienna. Until 1955, the Austrian capital, much like post-war Berlin, was divided into zones,

Rodower Strasse

Semmelweisstrasse

113

Wegedornstrasse

Rübezahlallee

Schönefelder Chaussee

Ortoffstrasse

Wegedornstrasse

COLD WAR
TUNNEL

Wolfmarsteig

113

Gerosteig

Germany

France

Mohnweg

Venusstrasse

Schönefelder Chaussee

Ortoffstrasse

Road tunnel

Secret tunnel

Buildings

0   500 metres

0   500 yards

Rail track

each controlled by the original four occupying Allied forces of France, Britain, the United States and the Soviet Union.

Spies at Rudow ultimately succeeded in tapping 172 phone lines and in all they logged some 443,000 conversations. Unbeknownst to them, however, there was a mole in their midst. George Blake, a British MI6 officer in Berlin, who'd taken minutes at meetings at which Operation Stopwatch was discussed, was a double agent. He'd been passing details of the scheme on to the KGB even before the ground for the tunnel was first broken, and on the night of 21 April 1956 the Soviets 'discovered' the tunnel. Seeking to capitalize (or perhaps communize) on the incident, they then held an international press conference to denounce the mendacity of the West. Which was a little rich since their own agents had already rigged up a tap at Potsdam on the American phone lines in West Berlin. In any event, the exposure of such a substantial bugging outfit did its perpetrators no real harm. In the West the tunnel and the mission itself were considered daring and were even admired for their ingenuity. Questions remain as to why the Soviets, in full possession of the facts, allowed the tapping to go on interrupted for a full eleven months. But most historians believe that they let the operation rumble on to prevent Blake, their valuable man on the inside, from being exposed. A section of the tunnel is open to visitors, along with the original Checkpoint Charlie, at the Allied Museum in Berlin, the city reunified since 1989.

Left: An East German soldier surveys the secret British and American listening post in a tunnel which extended into the Soviet-occupied zone of Berlin from the American side.

Beijing Underground

Bunkers to beat the bomb
Beijing [China]

39° 54' 27"N
116° 24' 15"E

After a decade of deteriorating relations between the most powerful, and neighbouring, communist nations on earth, Chinese and Soviet troops were embroiled in a series of skirmishes along the Soviet-Sino border in the spring of 1969. Like the Cuban missile crisis seven years earlier involving the Soviet Union and United States, this conflict, arising from disputes over territorial treaties signed in imperial and tsarist days, and the arguments over borders pre-dating those by centuries, brought the world to within a hair's breadth of nuclear war. Only assurances from the United States to Soviet officials that the USA would side with China in the event of an attack prevented the use of nuclear missiles on this occasion. The storm may have passed, but fear of future conflicts convinced Chairman Mao Zedong that China needed to be able to withstand a future nuclear assault.

Some four years earlier construction had begun on a new subway system for Beijing, ironically after Mao had visited Moscow and initially with the support of Russian engineers. This transport system was intended more for civil defence than commuting, and trials to see if its tunnels could handle nuclear bombardment were even held at Lop Nor, the Chinese atomic test site. But in the aftermath of the spat with the Soviets in 1969, work was now to begin on a complex of subterranean concrete bunkers with a secret network of interlinking escape tunnels snaking from Zhongnanhai, the Communist Party headquarters, out to the military bases beyond the city at Ba Da Chu. This Beijing Underground City, or Dixia Cheng, was planned with the eventual aim of accommodating all six million residents

Changping

Shunyi

Beijing
International
Airport

entougou

Shijingshan

Beijing

Tongzhou

Fengtal

ngshan

Daxing

● Subway Station
····· Subway line
▨ Urban area

China

0 _____ 10 kilometres

0 _____ 5 miles

– a target it's doubtful it ever met. The full extent of the sprawl of its supposedly nuclear fallout-proof concrete is unknown, but the tunnels under Tiananmen Square are rumoured to be large enough to allow tanks to pass through them and the network is thought to have reached an area of some 50 square miles.

In 2000 a tiny section of the tunnels was opened to the public, allowing visitors to step down into a realm that was as drably spartan as it was eldritch: picture a dank stairwell liberally decorated with faded propaganda posters

Below: Walls of the Beijing Underground decorated with Maoist art to remember those who dug and secured the tunnels.

advising citizens to cover their mouths against the effects of radiation. This time capsule of Mao's last years closed for 'restoration' in 2008; though much of Dixia Cheng is still intact, accessing it is both difficult and illegal, and parts have fallen to extensions to the Beijing subway system. Already the world's second largest, this is on course to double in size again before the decade is out, commerce and work triumphing over civil defence and war, it would seem.

MOOSE JAW

ILLICIT TUNNELS

SASKATCHEWAN [CANADA]

50° 23' 24" N
105° 32' 8" W

'History', the great German Jewish thinker Walter Benjamin once maintained, 'is written by the victors', and certainly for centuries victims of mad tyrants, unjust laws and oppressive regimes could expect little by way of redress in official records. The deeds of those without title were usually notable only by their absence in history books of old. Omission, though, can speak volumes. And almost every nation on earth has events from its past it would perhaps prefer to forget. Forgetting can in some rare instances be healthy. But history, no matter how painful, is vital for helping to forge a better future, ideally one where we don't make the same mistakes again. That said, sometimes it seems we never learn anything from the past.

Not so long ago in the 1970s, a decade in which social historians first seriously turned their attention to the lot of common and disenfranchised people in times past, officials in the Canadian city of Moose Jaw continued to deny rumours of a network of underground tunnels beneath their sleepy Saskatchewan metropolis. But when a section of the city's Main Street collapsed, plunging a passing car and its stunned driver several feet below ground and exposing a section of one subterranean passage to the scrutiny of all, such denials could no longer be sustained. The existence of the tunnels was, however, considered an embarrassment to the city. The story of their creation remains inextricably entwined with the passing of one of the most reprehensible laws in Canadian history: the Chinese head tax.

Canada has had a Chinese community for more than 150 years. The majority of the first Chinese migrants were drawn from Guangdong province to British Columbia, like thousands of others from elsewhere, by

Oxford St W

Oxford St E

Ross St W

Ross St E

Caribou St W

Caribou St E

Athabasca St W

Athabasca St E

Stadacona St W

3 Avenue NW

2 Avenue NW

1 Avenue NW

3 Avenue NE

Ominica St W

2

Moose Jaw

Fairford St W

Main Street N

Fairford St E

1 Avenue NE

High St W

High St E

2 Avenue NE

River St W

River St W

TUNNELS OF
MOOSE JAW

Capone's
Hideaway

363

Manitoba Street W

Canada

Main Street S

Rail track

Urban area

0   200 metres

Maple Street W   2   2   River Drive

0   200 yards

Home Street W   Home Street E

Above: Now a tourist attraction, a museum guide points to the long dark tunnels of Moose Jaw.

the promise of gold in the feverish rush of the late 1850s, a period when fortunes appeared to lie only a tin pan sift away for the luckiest of prospectors. Thirty years later, a new wave of Chinese came to Canada to work on the Canadian Pacific Railway. These newer arrivals were recruited directly from their homeland (or transplanted from California), as cheap labour by the railway's main contractor, the American Andrew Onderdonk. Chinese railway workers were paid on average about two-thirds the rate of white navvies and generally got a rougher deal altogether. They were given the riskiest, most backbreaking jobs on the construction of a route that required the blasting of tunnels through solid rock with dynamite – often in the bitter British Columbian winters.

If they expected any gratitude for their labours from Canadians once the railway was completed, they were to be disappointed. No sooner had they downed tools than the Canadian economy slipped into recession and unemployment shot up. The Chinese were accused of taking jobs from white Canadians and pushing down wages in what pitifully few positions were available. Labour unions and local politicians, pandering to prejudices for their own electoral advantage, called upon the Canadian government to impose restrictions on Chinese immigrants. More fuel was poured onto the fire by the gutter press, which ran salacious and racist articles about seedy opium dens and oriental super-villains and used editorials to spread hysteria about a supposed 'Yellow Peril' to the nation's way of life. In this toxic atmosphere, and to its eternal shame, the Canadian government caved in to public pressure in 1885 and imposed a $50 head tax on every Chinese person entering the country – a fee that applied to these nationals alone. However, it failed to stem the influx of new arrivals, Canada still seeming a better prospect for many than remaining a dirt-poor peasant in Imperial China. In 1900 the fee was doubled to $100 and three years after that upped to $500 – a sum about equal to two years' wages.

Relations between the Chinese and other residents across Canada remained tense and, it seems, in Moose Jaw especially so. In about 1908, a group of Chinese rail workers were set upon in one of the local yards by a gang of (possibly unemployed) white men. To avoid further attacks and evade the now exorbitant head tax, the Chinese went underground, quite literally digging tunnels beneath the city's streets to hole up in until things calmed down.

Over several years these tunnels, accessible from the basements of Chinese-owned businesses, spread into an expansive subterranean Chinatown that housed whole families of immigrants, most of whom worked illegally in the laundries or restaurants above their lairs.

The situation for Mandarin-speakers on Moose Jaw terra firma, however, was dealt a further blow in 1923 when the government passed the Chinese Immigration (or Exclusion) Act which prohibited virtually all Chinese immigration to Canada. This law also granted the police swingeing new powers to round up suspected illegal emigrants, and the legislation would last until 1947.

It was also in the 1920s that the Chinese appear to have cut a deal with the Mob, allowing them to use their tunnels for the storage and sale of bootleg liquor. Canada had adopted Prohibition as a largely temporary measure during the First World War. But in 1920, when most of its territories were gradually moving to repeal bans on alcohol, the neighbouring USA passed the Eighteenth Amendment outlawing intoxicating liquids. Moose Jaw, quietly out of the way of officers of the American law but directly linked to the States by the Canadian Pacific Railway, became something of a resort for Chicago gangsters. Al Capone and his right-hand man, Diamond Jim Brady – whose front teeth were studded with jewels and who always wore, locals recalled, impeccable grey suits – were not infrequent visitors to the tunnels. Poker games and girls for hire by then only added to their allure for gangsters from either side of the border. Shortly after this the tunnels seem to have fallen into a state of abeyance that was not corrected until they were restored and reopened to the public in the late 1990s.

Interestingly, J.G. Ballard, the Shanghai-born British novelist, was stationed with the RAF at the NATO air force base just outside Moose Jaw in 1953. It was there that he first encountered science fiction stories in pulp magazines in a city that he later dismissively described as a 'dead-end town with two filling stations and a bus depot'. But inspired by their depiction of 'a world of cars, offices, highways, airlines and supermarkets' that people 'actually lived in', Ballard began penning stories in the genre. All the more intriguingly, his first published novel, *The Wind From Nowhere*, though disowned by its creator as a piece of hack work almost as soon as it appeared in 1961, concerns a world ravaged by hurricane-force winds that drive the inhabitants of major cities to seek refuge in basements and underground tunnels.

CINCINNATI

ABANDONED SUBWAY

CINCINNATI, OHIO [UNITED STATES]

39° 6' 11"N
84° 30' 43"w

Just below the latest news, one of the first things that catches the eye of the Internet browser of Cincinnati's official website is a feed for traffic updates. 'Joe Nuxhall Way Reduced to Two Lane Thursday for Concrete Pour' and 'Emergency I-75 Lane Closure Scheduled for Friday Afternoon' ran the breaking items for this Ohioan city at the time of writing. The prominence given to this data is not especially unusual for an American city, nor indeed any city anywhere in the world. But the sense that it's all about the road and aimed squarely at motorists is hard to avoid. In line with many other prominent Midwestern cities like Detroit, Michigan and Indianapolis, Indiana, it has a proud history of car manufacturing, one that can be traced back to the opening of Ford's Walnut Hills plant for Model Ts in 1915. If Cincinnati made cars, among them the Chevrolet Impala, the Pontiac Firebird and the Buick Apollo, cars, in turn, would make the city: the interstate defining its east and west districts and ribbons of asphalt helping its suburban hinterland to grow far beyond the original downtown that mushroomed on a basin by the Ohio River and was encircled by seven hills.

But the course of its development could have taken a very different direction. Only a year after Ford set up shop, and at a point when electric street cars were carrying upwards of a million passengers around Cincinnati annually, the legislature voted to back the creation of a cross-city public subway system. The first setback was America's entry into the First World War, which delayed the start of its construction until 1920. By the time F. Scott Fitzgerald's *The Great Gatsby* was in the bookstores five years

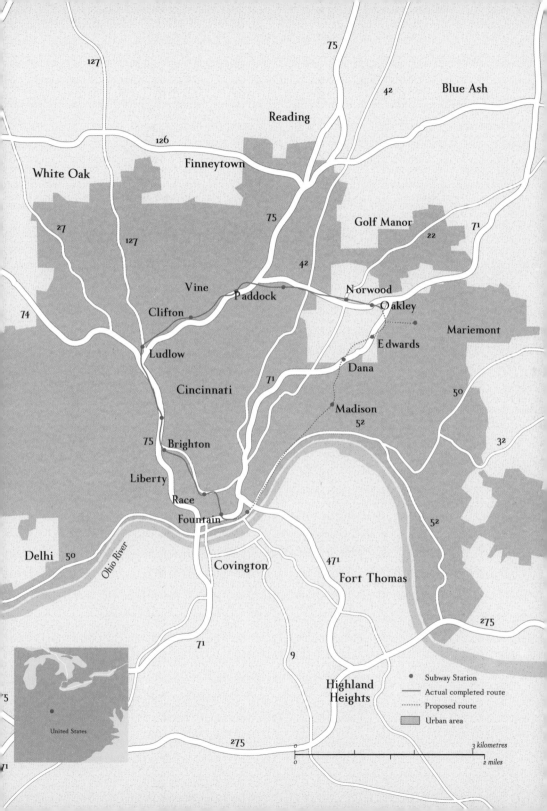

127

75

42

Blue Ash

126

Reading

White Oak

Finneytown

75

Golf Manor

7¹

²7

127

22

74

42

Vine

Norwood

Paddock

Oakley

Clifton

Mariemont

Ludlow

Edwards

Cincinnati

Dana

5⁰

7¹

Madison

75

Brighton

5²

3²

Liberty

Race

5²

Fountain

Delhi

5⁰

Ohio River

Covington

47¹

Fort Thomas

²75

7¹

9

Highland
Heights

●   Subway Station

─── Actual completed route

United States

········ Proposed route

         Urban area

⁷5

7¹

²75

0   3 kilometres

0   2 miles

later, nine miles of the system stood complete. Four subway stations and three surface stations were nearly done and dusted. There was, though, a worrying lack of track and rail stock. Worse still, the funding, hit badly by a post-war hike in inflation, was completely exhausted and construction that year came to an abrupt halt. While several attempts were made to rekindle the project, Cincinnati would, much like Daisy Buchanan spurning Gatsby after all his protracted wooing, choose to walk away from underground railway in the end. And with equally tragic results.

A little over two miles of tunnels, the largest abandoned subway in

America, stand intact to this day and some of its portals can be spied below sections of the traffic-clogged Central Parkway road. If its resurrection looks unlikely any time soon, Cincinnati at least appears to be repenting its earlier carelessness over public transportation. Streetcars are back in the city for the first time since 1951. The Cincinnati Bell Connector line linking the downtown area to the Over-the-Rhine district opened on 9 September 2016 – just in time for the centenary of the subway's own official birth.

ZKP Tagansky, aka Bunker 42

Cold War communications bunker
Moscow [Russia]

55° 44' 30"N
37° 38' 57"E

It is difficult to know which is more extraordinary: the fact that for an entrance fee of roughly $26 you can, in effect, launch a nuclear attack on the United States, or that two gentlemen of mature years earn their daily crust as lookalikes of, respectively, the former Soviet leaders Joseph Stalin and Leonid Brezhnev. Brezhnev is somewhat more convincing than Uncle Joe, it must be said. Playing an autocratic mass murderer rather than a man who merely engendered economic stagnation is probably a bigger ask of any impersonator, especially when you factor in Brezhnev's trademark eyebrows. But then almost everything about what was once called the Tagansky Protected Command Point, and is currently branded Bunker 42, is bound to be more than a little surreal.

A product of the Cold War at its frostiest, this former top-secret underground Soviet communication facility was completed in the Tagansky district of Moscow in 1956 and designed to survive an all-out thermonuclear attack. At street level its entrance remains discreet, tucked behind the corner of a modest neoclassical block and close to the Tagansky metro station which many of the 2,500-odd staff employed here at its peak relied upon to get to work, more often than not on special late-night trains. Situated 213 feet below ground to avoid the worst of any nuclear blast, and extending over 7,000 square feet, this bunker was equipped with everything to survive a post-apocalyptic event for ninety days, from stocks of food and an air recycling system to an artesian well for water and diesel generators for electricity.

Decommissioned in 2006 and sold to private enterprise with a keen

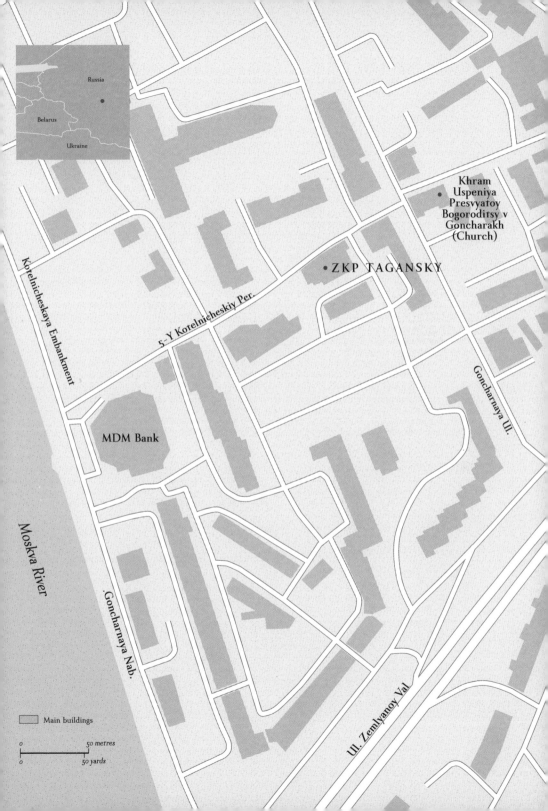

Russia

Belarus

Ukraine

Kotelnicheskaya Embankment

5-Y Kotelnicheskiy Per.

Khram
Uspeniya
Presvyatoy
Bogoroditsy v
Goncharakh
(Church)

• ZKP TAGANSKY

Goncharnaya Ul.

MDM Bank

Moskva River

Goncharnaya Nab.

Ul. Zemlyanoy Val

☐ Main buildings

0 ——— 50 metres
0 ——— 50 yards

understanding of the appeal of communist kitsch and the enduring appeal of somewhat nationalistic nostalgia, it has been transformed into an artefact-stuffed Soviet-period museum-cum-entertainment complex. Rooms that once hosted conferences for KGB members and fleets of telephone-monitoring operators have been transformed into concert halls for heavy metal bands and sumptuous (red or white themed) banqueting suites and (decidedly non-party political) party venues for wealthy Muscovites and their offspring. Wedding shindigs as well as live interactive role-playing games – some Iron Curtain-era historical, others dystopian and futuristic and involving paintballs and lasers and zombies – are all staged here. Those seeking a taste of the past or relatively mindless pleasure are accommodated with equal measure far below the streets of Moscow.

Left: Soviet-era equipment in Bunker 42. The once secret listening station can now be visited as part of the museum.

Puerto Princesa

_ _ _ _ _ _ _ _ _ _ _ _ _ _ _ _ _ _ _

Subterranean River

Palawan [Philippines]

10° 2' 42"n
118° 50' 13"e

Seven is often considered a lucky number. A prime number (one that cannot be divided by anything other than itself and one), it was referred to as the 'virgin' number by Pythagoras because it produced none of the first ten numbers and was not produced by any of them, and equated with the 'motherless' goddess Athena, who sprang from the head of Zeus. In the Bible, the world is created in seven days and a menorah with seven lamps illuminated the Temple in Jerusalem. We have seven days in a week and seven deadly sins. The list could go on, but one of the most captivating sevens to come down to us from the ancients was the Seven Wonders of the World – its canonical list containing two statues, a temple, a roof-top garden, two tombs and a lighthouse. Of these, only a single wonder remains, the Great Pyramid of Giza, i.e. one of the tombs of the pharoahs.

Herodotus, the so-called Father of History, is among those credited with originating the concept, though he could never have drawn up the final list since he lived in the fifth century, before three of the seven wonders were even built. The classic septet we have now was settled in the late Middle Ages, but it hasn't stopped people ever since from trying to knock sacred cows off their pedestals and replace them with others, or from composing contemporary variations along the same lines. In 1994, for example, the American Society of Civil Engineers drew up a Seven Modern Wonders of World, hailing the likes of the Golden Gate Bridge and the Channel Tunnel as feats of twentieth-century technical brilliance. And in 2007 a foundation based in Switzerland and calling itself New7Wonders of the World conducted a global poll to find, in its idiosyncratic spelling, the

SOUTH CHINA SEA

PUERTO PRINCESA
SUBTERRANEAN RIVER

Maratapi
Beach

Bentoan Beach

Cleopatra Needle

Botoon Beach

1450 m ▲
4712 ft

Ulugan Bay

Palawan

Fondeado
Island

Honda Bay

Fraser Island

Puerto
Princesa

Kalayaan
Beach

Phillipines

0   10 kilometres

0   5 miles

New7Wonders of Nature. One of the lucky seven was the Puerto Princesa Subterranean River in the Philippines.

Puerto Princesa, which was only first settled in 1874 and not incorporated as a city until ninety-six years later, is the bay-side capital of the Philippines island province of Palawan. It is composed of lots of little scattered rural villages, and only a third of its population live in the city per se. The Subterranean River lies within a national nature park some thirty miles to the north of the main metropolis. One whose claims of biodiversity, along with its mountainous scenery, tranquil lagoons and sandy beaches, is (with some justification) trumpeted in every guidebook and travel brochure going. The largest and most valuable limestone forest in Asia is to be found here. Said to be 'the longest navigable underground river in the world', the Subterranean River is a five-mile section of the Cabayugan River that runs underneath a mountain range and through a cave before heading directly out into the South China Sea: its waters, therefore, move from fresh to brackish as it approaches the ocean and are always subject to the push and pull of the tides.

Parts of the cave it passes through are up to 400 feet wide and nearly 200 feet high, but it's the rock formations produced by the river's ebb and flow which are so awesome. Centuries of briny water washing up against the limestone have left great accretions of speleothems along the sides and walls and roof of the cavern, rendering a journey through it rather like taking a spin inside a dragon's mouth. A wonder, in short, in anybody's language, and especially as eight different species of bat and an assortment of monitor lizards and hundreds of other varieties of flora and fauna, birds and reptiles thrive in its environs. We can only hope that, with a bit of luck, they are not adversely affected by the increasing number of visitors which its wonder status has attracted to this remarkable feature of the natural world.

Right: One of the New7Wonders of the World.

Select Bibliography

This book owes an enormous debt to numerous other books and articles. This select bibliography will, hopefully, give credit where credit is due and point those who want to know more in the right directions.

Aidala, Thomas R. *Hearst Castle, San Simeon*, Hudson Hill, New York, 1981.

Allen, Kristen. 'Euro Bridges: An Uncommon Monument to the Common Currency', Spiegel Online International, 4 November 2011

Aurand, Harold W. *Coalcracker Culture: Work and Values in Pennsylvania Anthracite, 1835–1935,* Susquehanna University Press: Selinsgrove and Associated University Presses: London, 2003.

Auroville: The First Six Years: 1968–1974, Auropublication, Auroville, 1974.

Butterworth, Mark. *Destination St. Kilda: From Oban to Skye and the Outer Hebrides*, Islands Book Trust, Isle of Lewis, 2010

Benjamin, Marina. *Rocket Dreams: How the Space Age Shaped Our Vision of a World Beyond*, Vintage, London, 2009.

Bennett Farmer, Sarah. *Martyred Village: Commemorating the 1944 Massacre at Oradour-sur-Glane*, University of California Press: Berkeley, Los Angeles and London, 1999.

Burke-Gaffne, Brian. 'Hashima: The Ghost Island', *Cabinet* magazine, Issue 7, 2002.

Campbell, Patricia J.; MacKinnon, Aran; and Stevens, Christy R. *An Introduction to Global Studies*, John Wiley, Chichester, 2010.

Cattermole, Paul. *Architectural Excellence: 500 Iconic Buildings*, Firefly Books, Richmond Hill ON, 2008.

Conley, Craig. *Puzzling Portmeirion: An Unconventional Guide to a Curious Destination*, Createspace, 2008.

Cooper, Richard, and Jackson, Dr Eric R. *Cincinnati's Underground Railroad*, Arcadia Publishing, Charleston SC, 2014.

Crick, Timothy. *Ramparts of Empire: The Fortifications of Sir William Jervois, Royal Engineer 1821–1897*. University of Exeter Press, Exeter, 2015.

Cronin, William B. *The Disappearing Islands of the Chesapeake*, Johns Hopkins University Press, Baltimore and London, 2005.

Dalton, Derek. *Dark Tourism and Crime*, Routledge: Abingdon and New York, 2015.

Darke, Diana, and Stewart, Murray. *North Cyprus*, Bradt Travel Guides, Chalfont St Peter, 2015.

Duncan, Andrew. *Secret London*, New Holland Publishers, London, 2006.

Elborough, Travis. *London Bridge in America: The Tall Story of a Transatlantic Crossing*, Jonathan Cape, London, 2013.

Elkins, T. H. with Hofmeister, B. *Berlin: The Spatial Structure of a Divided City*, Methuen, London and New York, 1988.

Fanthorpe, Lionel and Patricia. *The World's Most Mysterious Castles*, Dundurn, Toronto, 2005.

de Fortis, Paul, ed. *The Kingdom of Redonda, 1865–1990: A Celebration*, Aylesford, Wirral, 1991.

Freeman-Attwood, Marigold. *Leap Castle: A Place and Its People*, Michael Russell, Norwich, 2001.

Gillespie, Rosemary G., and Clague, David. *Encyclopedia of Islands*, University of California Press, Oakland, 2009.

Grathwol, Robert P.; Moorhus, Donita M.; and Steen, Gareth L. *Berlin and the American Military: A Cold War Chronicle*, New York University Press, New York and London, 1999.

Hadfield, Chris. *An Astronaut's Guide to Life on Earth*, Macmillan, London, 2015.

Hastings, Max. *Das Reich: The March of the 2nd SS Panzer Division Through France, June 1944*, Zenith Military Classics, London, 2013.

Hill, Ben. *Blue Murder: Two Thousand Doomed to Die. The Shocking Truth about Wittenoom's Deadly Dust*, Macmillan Sun Books, Melbourne, 1989.

Jorgensen, Anna, and Keenan, Richard, eds. *Urban Wildscapes*, Routledge, Abingdon and New York, 2012.

Karanian, Matthew. *Edge of Time: Traveling in Armenia and Karabagh*, Stone Garden Productions, Northridge CA, 2001.

Karanian, Matthew. *Historic Armenia After 100 Years: Ani, Kars, and the Six Provinces of Western Armenia*, Stone Garden Productions, Northridge CA, 2015.

Kastner, Victoria with a foreword by George Plimpton. *Hearst Castle: The Biography of a Country House*, Harry N. Abrams, New York, London, 2000.

Kirk, Ruth, and Alexander, Carmela. *Exploring Washington's Past: A Road Guide to History*, University of Washington Press, Washington DC, 1998.

Krane, Jim. *Dubai: The Story of the World's Fastest City*, Atlantic Books, London, 2009.

Lycett, Andrew. *The Man Who Created Sherlock Holmes: The Life and Times of Sir Arthur Conan Doyle*, Weidenfeld & Nicolson, London, 2007.

Maclean, Charles. *St. Kilda: Island on the Edge of the World*, Canongate, Edinburgh, 1972.

Macrakis, Kristie. *Seduced by Secrets: Inside the Stasi's Spy-Tech World*, Cambridge University Press, Cambridge and New York, 2008.

Miles, Malcolm. *Urban Utopias: The Built and Social Architectures of Alternative Settlements*, Routledge, Abingdon and New York, 2008.

Millard, Doug, ed. *Cosmonauts: Birth of the Space Age*, Scala, London, 2015.

Moreton, Cole. *Hungry for Home: Leaving the Blaskets. A Journey from the Edge of Ireland*, Viking, London, 2000.

Morris, Jan; Turner, Alwyn; Eastment, Mark; and Lacey, Stephen. *Portmeirion* Antique Collectors' Club, Woodbridge, 2006.

Motlagh, Jason. 'Slab City, Here We Come: Living Life Off the Grid in California's Badlands', *Time*, February 2012.

Murphy, David E.; Kondrashev, Sergei A.; and Bailey, George. *Battleground Berlin: CIA vs. KGB in the Cold War*, Yale University Press, New Haven, Conn. and London, 1997.

Nicholson, Geoff. *Walking in Ruins*, Harbour Books, Bath, 2013.

Nunez, Christina. 'Q&A: The First-Ever Expedition to Turkmenistan's "Door to Hell"', interview with George Kourounis, *National Geographic*, 17 July 2014.

Olsen, Brad. *Sacred Places Europe: 108 Destinations*, CCC Publishing, San Francisco, 2006.

Pattullo, Polly; Minelli, Orely; Hourmant, Patrick; Smith, Paul; Viesnik, Lee; and Dall, Amica. *The Ethical Travel Guide: Your Passport to Exciting Alternative Holidays*, Earthscan, Abingdon and New York, 2009.

Rattle, Alison, and Vale, Allison. *Hell House: And Other True Hauntings from Around the World*, Sterling, New York, 2005.

Rowell, Galen. *Poles Apart: Parallel Visions of the Arctic and Antarctic*, University of California Press, Oakland, 1997.

Sayre, Roger. *From Space to Place: An Image Atlas of World Heritage Sites on the 'in Danger' List*, World Heritage Series, UNESCO Publishing, Paris, 2012.

Shomette, Donald. *Lost Towns of Tidewater Maryland*, Schiffer Publishing, Atglen PA, 2010.

Smookler, Charles. *Colma*, Images of America, Arcadia Publishing, Charleston SC, 2007.

Stagles, Joan, and Stagles, Ray. *The Blasket Islands: Next Parish America*, O'Brien Press, Dublin, 2006.

Steel, Tom. *The Life and Death of St. Kilda*, HarperCollins, London, 2011.

Twitchell, James B. *Winnebago Nation: The RV in American Culture*, Columbia University Press, New York, 2014.

Williams-Ellis, Clough. *Portmeirion: The Place and Its Meaning*, Blackie & Son, Edinburgh, 1973.

To my wife Emily, for joining me on the journey

ACKNOWLEDGEMENTS

Thanks first to Lucy Warbuton at Aurum for approaching me with the idea of compiling an 'atlas of impossible places' to begin with. We settled on 'improbable' eventually, which made life a little easier, though I imagine I was probably still pretty impossible to work with. And to Richard Collins who diligently copy-edited the text that emerged as a result of Lucy's patient coaxing and my labours. Thanks to Alan Horsfield, my collaborator on this project, who supplied the wonderful maps.

Thanks to the staff and librarians at The British Library in St Pancras and The London Library in St James's. And in addition I'd like to thank: Nick Rennison, Alex Mayor, Julius Beltrame, Helen Gordon, Christian Flamm, Paul Kelly, Debsey Wykes, Bob Stanley, Pete Wiggs, Martin Kelly, Cathi Unsworth, Syd Moore, Ken Worpole, Liz Vater, Pete Brown, Dusty Miller, Joe Kerr, Charles Holland, John Rogers, my folks and family on either side of the atlantic and my beautiful and brilliant wife, Emily Bick.

PICTURE CREDITS

INDEX

Brimming with creative inspiration, how-to projects and useful information to enrich your everyday life, Quarto Knows is a favourite destination for those pursuing their interests and passions. Visit our site and dig deeper with our books into your area of interest: Quarto Creates, Quarto Cooks, Quarto Homes, Quarto Lives, Quarto Drives, Quarto Explores, Quarto Gifts, or Quarto Kids.

First published in 2016 by Aurum Press
an imprint of The Quarto Group
The Old Brewery
6 Blundell Street
London N7 9BH
www.QuartoKnows.com

This edition first published in 2017
© Quarto Publishing plc. 2016, 2017
Text © Travis Elborough 2016

Map illustrations by Alan Horsfield

Every effort has been made to trace the copyright holders of material quoted in this book. If application is made in writing to the publisher, any omissions will be included in future editions.

A catalogue record for this book is available from the British Library.

ISBN 978 1 78131 763 1
Ebook ISBN 978 1 78131 635 1
10 9 8 7 6 5 4 3 2 1
2021 2020 2019 2018 2017

Designed by Nick Clark and Paul Oakley, www.fogdog.co.uk
Printed in Hong Kong